THE LUCKY BAG

Opening Old Memories

Other Publications

The War Within (2011)

Sinjinlands (2011)

THE LUCKY BAG

Opening Old Memories

By Gerard J. St. John

Cover Photographs:

Front: Sampan leaving Hong Kong Harbor (October 1962)

Back: Gerard J. St. John and his daughter Monique Dougherty (July 2015)

Table of Contents

FOREWORD

"Lucky Bag" is a nautical term. I first heard it in the Marine Corps. A lucky bag is not a bag at all. It is a large locker into which are placed those various and sundry things that are left lying around a ship. You might call it the ship's "lost & found" department. At the end of each voyage – sometimes sooner – the lucky bag is opened and the men have a chance to identify and reclaim their property. I like the concept of the lucky bag.

In the 1990s, when e-mail messages came into being, I quickly labeled one of my file folders "lucky bag," and use it to archive messages that do not fit in with my established files. For example, it is where I file my orders from amazon.com and also where I store my passwords.

My writings are saved on a USB flash drive that hangs at the end of a gray lanyard in my home office. In many respects, that flash drive is my digital lucky bag. It contains reminiscences, bits and pieces of thoughts that interested me along the way – I call them random passages – a couple of historical articles about places in Northeast Philadelphia, a half-dozen or so legacy tributes that recall the passing of friends over the years. There are even a few attempts at poetry.

Finally, there are a few "letters" addressed to my friend Harry Silcox, stating my thoughts on some of Harry's historical articles. I don't expect Harry to respond to those letters. He died in 2009. However, the letters preserve the types of conversations that we used to have about local history.

I don't know whether or not this journey is nearing its end, but let's open the lucky bag and see what we find.

This verse was written in 1965 to accompany a gaudy orange and purple tie that Mary Kilroy and Janet Toohey purchased for Frank Mulligan on the occasion of Frank leaving his employment at the Redevelopment Authority to attend Temple University School of Law. The original document has been lost over the years. After fifty years, I cannot recall the exact words, but this is a close approximation.

MULLIGAN'S TIE

By the curb of far north Broad Street,

By the steaming blacktop roadway,

At the doorway of the Law School,

In the muggy summer morning,

Francis Mulligan stood and waited.

All the air was slightly noxious.

All the earth was less than joyous.

And before him, through the smog bank,

Westward, toward the neighboring jungle,

Passed in motley swarms, the Students,

Passed the owls, the money-makers,

Weeping, wailing, of their test marks.

From the brow of novice Darrow,

Gone is every trace of sorrow;

As the cop from out the red car,

As the con from out of Moko.

High above him shines a red light,

Orange spread his shoes before him;

From our hands receive this present,

Sparkling, flashing free from fashion.

A SHIBE PARK MEMORY

It was the summer of 1949, and I was just twelve years old. In retrospect, it is hard to believe that I was allowed to go by myself to a night baseball game at 21st and Lehigh Avenue. However, the Phillies were playing the St. Louis Cardinals and the Cardinals, led by Marty Marion at shortstop and Stan Musial at first base, were my favorite non-Philadelphia team.

From my standpoint it was a great game. The Phillies were hitting that night, and by the seventh inning they pretty much had the game wrapped up. Curt Simmons was pitching for the Phils. Curt was a young guy, a lightning quick lefthander barely out of his teens. It was late. I was tired; and I was tempted to join the exodus of fans who were leaving the ball park to get an early start home. Then, I looked at the scorecard. In the ninth inning, Stan Musial would come to bat again against Curt Simmons. I had to wait.

When the ninth inning rolled around, I got up and walked to the exit behind my upper deck seat. I would watch Simmons and Musial from that spot, and then get a running start to the No. 54 trolley regardless of the outcome. In my mind's eye, I can still see that confrontation, the league's best left-handed hitter against the league's best left-handed pitcher, with two outs in the ninth inning. Simmons struck him out. Musial swung at the last pitch but never touched it.

Tonight, an online obituary said that Stan Musial rarely struck out – never as many as 50 times in a season. I would love to have a photo of that graceful swing at Curt's last pitch in the summer of 1949. On the other hand, a photograph could never have the balance and beauty of that memory.

I'll never forget it.

A DIFFERENT KIND OF MARTYRDOM

On March 15, 1958, the St. Joseph's College basketball team played St. Bonaventure in the quarterfinal round of the National Invitation Tournament in New York City. In those days, the NIT was a major post-season basketball tournament; some people said that it was "the" major tournament. It was held in the old Madison Square Garden on Eighth Avenue, at 50th Street. The 18,000-seat "Garden" was a great sports venue. It was right out of Damon Runyon; and so were some of the regulars who inhabited the smoke-filled recesses of that hallowed site. Adding to the attraction in 1958 was the fact that the game was being played on Saturday night of the St. Patrick's Day weekend. We took an early afternoon train to New York. When we boarded the train at 30th Street Station, Sadie Haughton was especially excited. He said that I would get to meet "the Bagel." I had no idea what he was talking about.

After the train pulled into New York's Penn Station, we walked several blocks to a small Irish pub. It was late in the afternoon – too early for the game. "He said to meet him here," said Sadie. Near the front of the establishment, in a booth by himself, was a man in his early 30s (which, at the time, we considered to be middle age), wearing an old-time baseball jacket, the kind that had a woolen body and leather sleeves. He was holding a black cigar. It was Reverend Robert H. Breen, a recently ordained priest with the curious nickname "Bagel."

During the summers of his last few years in the seminary, Breen worked as a counselor at the Gwynned Mercy Day Camp. Counselors were expected to reward successful campers with tokens of victory in the daily games. Some counselors awarded ribbons; others awarded medals or coins. The token was left to the discretion of the individual counselor. No one told Bob Breen of that expectation until his first morning at the camp. Breen then scurried around the camp like a kid on a scavenger hunt, looking for some trinkets that he could use to recognize the victors in that morning's events. There was nothing in sight. Then, he went into the kitchen, and there was a bag of bagels. Bagels became both his award and his life-long nickname.

At the Irish pub, Sadie introduced him to me as "Bagel." I said, "That is all I have heard for the past two hours on the train." He replied, "All I have heard for the past week is that I was going to meet the Saint." We talked for about an hour or so and then walked over to the

THE BAGEL, FR. BOB BREEN

Garden where we went our separate ways. Bagel reminded me of

the priest played by Bing Crosby in the popular movie, *The Bells of St. Mary's.*

The following year, after graduation from St. Joe's, I went into the Marines. From September 1959 through June 1960, I was stationed at Marine Corps Schools, Quantico, Virginia. During that stretch, I spent most of my spare time in Philadelphia and at the Jersey shore. I knew that in June I would probably be transferred to a distant Marine Corps base. Still, Sadie insisted that I join him and a group of friends in renting a house for the summer in Ocean City, New Jersey. Obie O'Brien organized the group and named it "Chez Dix" (house of ten), even though there were twelve of us involved. Obie graduated from La Salle High a year or so behind me. Approximately half of the Chez Dix group was from St. Joe's and the other half was from La Salle College. The La Salle people were about a year younger than the St. Joe contingent. That meant that most of them were too young to be served at the nearby drinking establishments, a fact that we knew would cause us problems. The oldest member of Chez Dix was our chaplain, Father Bob Breen – the Bagel.

I was right at home with the concept of a chaplain. Chaplains are a traditional part of the military, dating back to the English navy more than one thousand years ago. Typically, the chaplain is a priest who provides support for the spiritual and emotional needs of the crew. As chaplain of Chez Dix, Bagel had his work cut out for him. It wasn't long before Bagel's practical skills came into play. One of the younger members of the house frequently found himself in the clutches of law enforcement officials of the neighboring town of Margate, New Jersey. The typical fine for underage drinking in Margate was about $100. That was a lot of money at that stage of our lives. We sympathized with our friend's predicament, but most of us thought that he created the problem, and that he was the one who should resolve it. Bagel stepped into the breach.

Bagel was about ten years older than most of us. He graduated from La Salle High in the closing days of World War II. He attended classes at Pennsylvania Maritime Institute, which prepared him for a career in the merchant marine. During his second year at the Maritime Institute, he signed on with the merchant marines. To hear Bagel tell the story, you would think of John Wayne and the U.S. Marines on the *Sands of Iwo Jima*. In fact, he was the purser on a cruise ship. Soon he heard the call to the priesthood and entered St. Charles Seminary. During his hitch in the merchant marines, he gained some practical experience in dealing with personnel problems. The ship's crew stuck together. If money was lost or stolen, each member of the crew would throw $10 into a pot to help refinance the loser. The crew members would not miss the ten-spot, and although the amount collected would not be as great as the loss, the victim would be restored to solvency and would feel like a part of a cohesive team. It was a good remedy.

On the other hand, repeat offenders tend to generate a good bit of resentment. When we saw Obie on the beach in the morning going from person to person, we knew that Hank had done it again, and we began to grumble. I probably grumbled less than my cohorts. My allotted time on the East Coast was coming to an end. I was shipping out. My orders called for me to report to Camp Pendleton, California by the second week of August 1960.

My last two weeks at the Jersey Shore bore little resemblance to the festive "farewell tours" of present-day athletes, but it was a fun time. However, on my last day in Ocean City, when I pulled up to Chez Dix to pick up my gear, there was a noticeable chill in the air. "What's up?" I asked. "Bagel's leaving," was the terse reply. "He's upset because we let Nancy McGinn sleep on the porch last night when her girlfriends left Ocean City without her. She had no place to stay." "Bagel's upstairs packing his bags." I decided to take a walk upstairs.

Bagel was in the front room. A small suitcase lay open on the bed. Bagel's eyes were fixed on an open dresser drawer. He did not look up as I entered the room. "Father Breen (I rarely addressed him as 'Bagel'), I thought that I was the one who is leaving." "I can't stay here, Saint, not after last night. They let a girl stay in the house overnight. Everyone knows that I'm a priest. We set the rules at the start. No women were to stay in the house. I have to insist on that rule." "Well Father, I just heard about this

9

a few minutes ago – but what I heard sounds a lot different." I was tempted to say, "That was no girl; that was Joe's sister." But I did not say that. I said, "Nancy always stops over here to talk to Joe and the rest of the guys. She is like family. She had no place to stay. It was late. What were they to do? Besides, it was not like they gave her one of the bedrooms; they let her stay on the front porch."

Father Breen turned around and looked at me, but he did not say anything. He was thinking. I pushed it a bit farther. "It seems to me that you serve a real purpose here. Issues like this are going to come up whether you are here or not. This group is going to be a whole lot better off if they have your guidance. Isn't that what being a chaplain is all about?"

At that point, I reminded the Bagel that I had to leave for Camp Pendleton. I bade my farewell and added, "I hope that you change your mind and stay." I never did hear what transpired after I left, but I have the strong impression that the Chez Dix chaplain served his full tour of duty that summer.

Three years later, when I returned to the East Coast, things had changed. My Chez Dix T-shirt was long gone. It was shredded by the underbrush on the island of Okinawa. Most of the ten – or twelve – members of our 1960 seashore house were now married and pursuing their own lives. Chez Dix existed only in our memories.

On occasion, I would hear stories about Father Breen. He was a teacher at Cardinal Dougherty High School in Olney (at the time, the largest Catholic high school in the world); he was the golf coach at La Salle College; he was a parish priest at St. Anne's in Port Richmond or a pastor in rural Riegelsville; he was the chaplain for the teams in Philadelphia's Big-5 Basketball program – and at one point for the Philadelphia Eagles football team. On rare occasion, we had passing contact. At the conclusion of Sadie Haughton's funeral Mass, Father Breen glanced at the pallbearers and said, "It looks like the Chez Dix." There were similar comments at the wedding of Jim Gavaghan's daughter Maureen and Scott Arnold, a member of Breen's La Salle golf team.

It did not occur to me at the time, but a chaplain's social circle is often defined by the boundaries of his current crew. During the course of the chaplaincy, there is close contact between the crew and the chaplain. Members of the crew seek out the chaplain to officiate at their weddings, and to baptize their first born. When the chaplain moves on to another assignment, he slowly loses contact with the earlier group. A few years ago when Father Breen reached retirement age, he was assigned to Villa St. Joseph, the priests' retirement home in Darby. In retirement, Father Breen helped out with the weekend Masses at St. Andrew the Apostle Church in Drexel Hill – my parish. My contact with the chaplain had come full circle.

Bagel now added my name to the list of people he could call when he needed a ride. Rides became a frequent need when Bagel's declining health made him give up his car. A retirement home is not a pleasant place for someone who is accustomed to a high level of social activity. Many of the retired priests are in poor physical or mental health, and they live in their own tightly circumscribed worlds. For active priests like Bagel, the urge to get away is overwhelming.

One of Bagel's getaways is the weekly lunch of the Markward Club, the group that supports high school basketball in the Philadelphia area. Bagel is the unofficial chaplain of the club. Invariably, he is asked to say grace before meals. He jokes about the time that a lunch occurred on Ash Wednesday, and the club arranged for him to have an adjoining room where he distributed ashes to people who attended the luncheon. Ash Wednesdays present Bagel with a different challenge. He is a picky eater. On the fourth day of creation, God did not create a single fish that Bagel believes is edible. Vegetables? Father Breen's nephews insist that as a child he was attacked by a carrot and a bunch of broccoli. His penance on Ash Wednesdays is to have scrambled eggs for all three meals. The Markward Club also gives the aging chaplain a chance to re-connect with some of his former charges from years gone by: Billy Oakes, a St. Joe guard and NBA referee; Herb Magee, the hall-of-fame basketball coach; Joe Heyer, the sharpshooting guard from La Salle; Don Di Julia, St. Joe's athletic director; Fran Dunphy who now coaches at Temple; and a host of other people from the past.

In retrospect, Bagel could not have picked a worse time for his retirement. It coincided with a series of Philadelphia grand jury reports that accused many priests of sexual abuse crimes against juveniles dating back to the 1940s. That evil was compounded by the poor judgment of archdiocesan officials who failed to confront and deal forthrightly with the criminals. Sensationalized publicity gave the impression that all Catholic priests are hiding their own past acts of sexual abuse. These are trying times for an old chaplain who served his flock with distinction for more than 50 years, and always confronted his crew when it was going astray. Now, like many other Catholic priests, Bagel is being viewed with suspicion by people who never had any contact with him.

In contrast, those of us who have known Bagel for many years recognize his contributions to our lives. He is a member of La Salle High's hall of fame. The Cardinal Dougherty High School Alumni Association dedicates its annual golf tournament to Father Breen in recognition of his "56 years in the priesthood and for all he has done for both the Cardinal Dougherty Community and the church in the Delaware Valley." The archdiocese did not help this exemplary priest when they housed many of the abuser-priests in a "prayer and penance" program in Villa St. Joseph, thereby forcing Bagel to live side-by-side with the malefactors who disgraced him and all other priests. Moving out of the Villa to a private dwelling place is not an option because a priest's retirement compensation is minimal and even that small sum is being reduced by an archdiocese that is trying to cut expenses in all areas.

On Thursday afternoons, Father Breen and I get together with a group that Bagel calls "The Old Geezers." It is a group of about 15 retired men, most of whom had some connection with high school athletics in the 1940s and 1950s. The youngest member was one of Father Breen's students at Cardinal Dougherty High School in the 1960s. The topics of discussion vary widely. As befits a chaplain, Father Breen rarely criticizes any particular individual. Similarly, he rarely comments on the failings of the archdiocese or his fellow priests. Not long ago, he was asked point-blank what it was like to be a long-term priest living in the shadow of the sex abuse scandal where many members of the public wrongly assume that every priest is a sexual abuser. Bagel hesitated for a moment, and then summed up his thoughts in one short sentence:

"It is a different kind of martyrdom."

YOU ARE MY SUNSHINE

It is one of those songs that everyone knows. They know the tune, and they know the words.

> You are my sunshine,
>
> My only sunshine.
>
> You make me happy
>
> When skies are gray.
>
> You'll never know dear
>
> How much I love you.
>
> Please don't take my sunshine away.

The song is a mixture of sunshine and sadness. It was introduced at the advent of the Second World War. At that time I did not fully understand the emotional aspects of the tune. I was barely four years old when it came out. Still, the song remained popular throughout the war years and beyond.

When the war finally ended, I was eight years old. My northeast Philadelphia neighborhood was like a continuing construction site, meeting the demand created by the return of several million soldiers to civilian life. Thousands of new homes were being built and promptly sold, assisted by federal funds made available under the law that people called the "G-I Bill of Rights." When you are eight years old, you think that things are preordained to happen the way they did. You think that prosperity and peace are inseparable. You think that grown-ups really know what they are doing.

I attended a parochial grammar school. My school was St. Matthew's, on Cottman Avenue at Hawthorne Street. With the end of the war, attendance at St. Matthew's increased geometrically. In first grade there were 32 boys in our class. A separate girls' class had about the same number. But two classes behind us, the numbers doubled – and it was not long before the numbers doubled again. St. Matt's needed more classrooms. A second floor was added, and then a new classroom wing in the back. The church building was expanded. A convent was added – and a rectory. When we sat in the classroom and looked dreamily out the windows, we were usually looking at stone masons working on the current project.

Classes were taught by Sisters of the Immaculate Heart of Mary, which we later called "IHMs." We thought that there was an inexhaustible supply of nuns. Similarly, there were a lot of priests assigned to St. Matthew's. We were told that ours was an emerging generation that would lead the world in the post-war era. Maybe that is why we were not terribly surprised when Robert Sinush joined our eighth-grade class in the new school building. Robert was big. He was two years older than the rest of us, and he had difficulty with the English language. He was a "DP," a displaced person from Lithuania. He had been separated from his family by the war, and was trying to blend into America with the help of a Lithuanian-American community in Schuylkill County.

However, for the next year, Robert would live with a family in our neighborhood and would be a part of our eighth-grade class. The goal was for Robert to become more accustomed to American life, so that he could transition smoothly into his new surroundings in Schuylkill County. A few members of the class were assigned to help Robert in specific areas of his class work. I was asked to help with his understanding of mathematics. It was not a difficult task. We generally spent about thirty minutes each morning reviewing our math assignments. During breaks in our normal class routine, we spent a lot of time talking about the things that interested eighth graders.

Robert spoke with a deep guttural accent that was similar to the speech patterns of our neighbors who were of German or Polish extraction. His vocabulary was good. We had no trouble understanding him, nor did he have any trouble understanding us. It was just a matter of smoothing out some linguistic rough spots. We were fascinated by his stories about growing up in a war zone. He said that you could hear the distant roar of airplane engines long before you could see the planes. The roar would get louder and louder, and then there were rows and rows of planes flying overhead. The Allied planes would continue overhead on their way to targets in Germany. On occasion, there would be German fighter planes attacking nearby troop concentrations, and even strafing women and children who tried to run to safety. On one such occasion, Robert's aunt was struck and killed by the bullets from those planes. The stories brought home the reality of war.

By and large, Robert got along well with his new classmates — that is all except Rich Sauerbaum. I don't know what was wrong with Rich. In retrospect, he may have suffered from a medical problem. His facial expression always looked like he just bit into a lemon. To make matters worse, he was quick to start yelling, and also quick to start throwing punches. He was constantly getting into fights. It wasn't that he was tough. He usually lost the fights. But he continued to provoke them. One afternoon, as we were filing out the back door of the classroom, Rich shouted something at Robert and then followed it up with a push, and then a punch. Rich must have forgotten that he was picking on someone who was two years older and about twenty pounds heavier than he. Robert threw one punch, and it sent Rich sprawling down the side of the room. The fight was over. It was the only time that I saw Robert angry.

On one of the last days of that school year, Robert came into class with a big smile on his face. Looking right at me, he said, "I heard a song on the radio last night. It was about you!" Then, he started singing "You are my sunshine." "You are sunshine," he repeated. I didn't know what to say, so I just laughed along with him. That was more than sixty years ago.

The other night, I was watching television. Turner Classic Movies featured the George Clooney film, "Oh Brother, Where Art Thou?" Near the end of the show, the governor grants a pardon to Clooney's "Soggy Bottom Boys," and they celebrate with a rousing chorus of "You Are My Sunshine."

It brought back a distant memory. I wonder what happened to that old black-and-white photo of my grammar school class?

RED CARS IN THE SUNSET

One of the highlights of being in seventh grade was membership in the "Safety Patrol," the students who assisted in maintaining order at the start and finish of each school day. Safeties got to wear a military style Sam Brown belt, one of those configurations that looped across your body and over the shoulder. It had an official looking "Safety" badge in the middle of the chest area. Some safeties were assigned to the schoolyard where each class lined up in a column of twos, and to the street corners where students entered and exited the school premises. Other safeties accompanied a class to the street intersection where those students left the school property. Along with one of my classmates, I was assigned to the southwest corner of Cottman and Hawthorne Streets, which had the heaviest vehicular traffic on the boundary of St. Matthew's School.

The City of Philadelphia also recognized the need for pedestrian traffic control at that intersection. In addition to a traffic light, two policemen were assigned to the intersection in the morning, at lunch time, and at dismissal in the afternoon. We got to know those policemen pretty well. They insisted that we call them by their first names, Harry and Frank. That was a big deal when you were in seventh grade.

Typically, we would arrive at the intersection at about the same time as the patrol car. In the 1940s, all Philadelphia police cars were bright red. No private cars were colored red. If you saw a red car, you knew immediately that it was a policeman. In fact, the common nickname for "police car" was "red car." Some policemen did not like that color association. They thought that it prevented them from blending in with the other cars on the street. Maybe some of them just did not like the color red. On the other hand, when Harry and Frank parked their red car near the traffic light on Cottman Avenue, all motorists were on notice that the traffic laws would be strictly enforced at that intersection.

Harry and Frank stayed with us for about twenty minutes at noon, and again at our 3:30 pm dismissal. Harry was on the short side, slender, and wore a thin moustache. He was full of questions about our classroom life; and he had no hesitation in sharing his thoughts about his police routine. Frank joined in the conversation but he was less talkative than Harry. We enjoyed those daily street corner sessions but, like most kids, we welcomed the arrival of summer vacation despite the fact that it brought our safety patrol duties to an end.

I don't know what brought about the change that summer, but a gambling craze set in on the neighborhood. Maybe it was a result of the "older guys" being in high school. Whatever the cause, it seemed like betting dominated our every activity. Bets were made at the start of neighborhood touch football games and baseball games. Usually, the bets revolved around the number of points scored. Pretty soon, the games ended when it became clear who would win the bet rather than who would win the game. Also, there were card games, mainly blackjack and poker. We played for pennies, nickels, dimes and quarters.

In the present day and age where drug dealers exchange thousands of dollars on street corners and life savings are regularly lost in casinos, penny ante blackjack games are small time things. However, we grew up in the 1940s – and in the 1940s, the only allowable forms of gambling were the 50-50 drawings of charitable organizations and the parish BINGO games. In those days, when people saw children gambling – no matter what the stakes – they called the police to end what they considered to be a public nuisance. Although I did not like gambling on sporting events, I was fascinated by the mathematical principles that applied to most games of chance. Moreover, I owned a deck of cards.

One afternoon, Don Donaghy and I sat down on the curb next to Mr. Boger's house at the end of the block, and began a game of blackjack. We put our pennies and nickels in the open dirt space between the curb and the sidewalk. One or two of our friends came by and joined the game. I was doing pretty well, about fifty cents ahead. It was then that the "older guys" came around, Jack Donaghy and Bob Regan. After that, the stakes became higher – no more penny bets. Then, someone looked up and saw a red car cruise slowly by the corner of Oakmont Street. The game was over – or at least postponed. We went around the corner to Chippendale Avenue and set up shop by the front door of the Donaghys' house, about midway up the block. We were partially hidden from view by the shrubbery on the front lawn. The game resumed and the amounts of the bets increased. My luck had changed. I was not doing well.

I was seated against the front wall of the Donaghys' house, looking down the walk toward the street. I was the first one to see the red car pull up next to the sidewalk. I quietly warned the others, and then slowly eased myself back and away from the money and the cards. The other players started to do the same thing but by that time, the two policemen were upon us. The policemen directed their attention to the two oldest players, Bob Regan and Jack Donaghy.
"What is your name?"
"Where do you live?"

One of the policemen, the slender one with the thin moustache, picked up all the money that was lying on the ground. He separated out the pennies and handed them to the youngest child in the small group that had gathered to watch the card game. He gave the nickels to another child. Then, he took all of the remaining money, and with an imperceptible wink, handed it to me. Bob Regan could not restrain himself. He cried out, "He's giving the money to Gerry — and he started the game!" In my mind, it was poetic justice.

CARL BUCK

The memories start about 66 years ago, when you moved to the 3300 block of Chippendale Avenue, a new row of houses.

Even then, you were tall; I was, let's say, "vertically challenged."

Our turf included the Victory Gardens, the Poor Farm and the Pennypack Woods. The driveway behind your house was a neighborhood highway to Kanes Market at the far end of the block; our parents saw each other every day and knew each other well.

You, Don and I walked the long mile to St. Matt's School – back and forth at lunchtime – and again at the end of the day. We went separate ways in high school; but we stayed friends. You thought that you were tough when you joined the Marines; and maybe you were. You hated it and often wished that you did not have to take that bus back to Camp Lejeune.

You needled me when I joined the Corps, albeit offering solid support when no one else was listening.

Life's a blur; I saw you only once in the last 50 years or so. Has it really been that long?

There are so many memories.   Semper Fi!

A TIME FOR HEROES

Early last week, Father Robert Breen called and asked what I was doing on Thursday. He needed a ride to St. Albert the Great Church for the funeral of Tom Gola. Of course I would attend Tom Gola's funeral. He was one of my heroes.

It has been nearly 65 years since I first heard the name Tom Gola. I was a freshman at La Salle High School; Tom was a

senior. Everyone at La Salle knew Tom Gola – or at least it seemed that way. He was a tall, slender young man who fit in well with his classmates. He was at the top of his class in academics, and in a class by himself on the basketball court. I did not follow basketball at that time, but I was impressed by Gola's athletic ability playing softball. He hit a softball farther than anyone I ever saw.

Toward the end of my freshman year, two Tom Gola stories swept through the La Salle campus. The first story had to do with an award ceremony for the outstanding high school basketball players in the Philadelphia area. It was one of the few times that the all-stars of the Catholic and Public Leagues were honored at a single formal event. It was a "coat and tie" affair at one of the downtown hotels. One of those outstanding high-schoolers lived in a poverty-stricken neighborhood. He did not own either a coat or a tie. To attend the award dinner, he borrowed a suit from one of his uncles, a rather large uncle. The baggy suit was embarrassing. He looked like a clown. When it came time to take group photographs, the poorly clad player was nowhere to be found.

His teammates knew where he was hiding, but they were reluctant to call further attention to their friend. Instead, they went to Tom Gola, saying, "You are the only one he will listen to." Tom found the player hiding in a restroom, and persuaded him to join in the group photos, albeit in the back row where his borrowed clothes would not be apparent. It was the kind of thing we had come to expect from Tom Gola.

The second story had to do with college scholarships. Gola received offers of scholarships from nearly 100 colleges and universities across the nation. Rumor had it that some of those offers were coupled with amenities that would give him spending money and his own car. Tom surprised everyone by accepting the scholarship offered by La Salle College. Also included in the deal were scholarships for his two brothers. Tom would attend college (and play basketball) on the same campus where he attended high school.

In my sophomore year, I made it a point to attend some of the high school's basketball games. Gradually, I learned something about the sport, including the speed and endurance required of basketball players. On the other hand, I knew little or nothing about the background of the sport. In particular, I did not know that in 1951 several prominent New York colleges and players were banned from basketball competition because they conspired with gamblers to control the point-spread in specific games. Their teams won those games — but by less than the predicted point differential. The gamblers collected big money from their bets, and rewarded the players with cash payments. It was called the "point-shaving" scandal. New York basketball fans were devastated. They had no New York teams to rally behind, and that was a rare circumstance in the Big Apple.

In the meanwhile, the prohibition against freshmen playing on varsity teams was suspended for the duration of the war in Korea, enabling Tom Gola to lead La Salle College to the championship of the National Invitation Tournament in New York City. It seemed as though a love affair developed between the New York news media and Tom Gola. Philadelphia basketball fans made it a regular practice to drive up to Madison Square Garden to watch Tom Gola play against well-known New York teams and other national powers. Madison Square Garden on Eighth Avenue was the "Holy Grail" of basketball. The Philadelphians met at the Taft Hotel for a few beers prior to the game, walked to "the Garden," and eventually found their way back to Philadelphia. On the return trips, the conversations invariably centered on how well Tom Gola played that night.

Back at La Salle, the high school and the college continued to share the same basketball court. The high school held its practices early in the afternoon, after which the college took possession of the gym. On occasion, the college team scrimmaged against the local NBA team, the Philadelphia Warriors. Rumor had it that the college team prevailed in many of those battles. The temptation was overwhelming. I joined a group of students who hung around the gym when the high school's practice ended. The college officials made sure that all unauthorized persons left the premises, and then they locked the doors. Fortunately, they did not close the interior window that was located high on the wall at one end of the court. Seven or eight of us went up the stairway and watched the scrimmages from the landing behind that window.

Basketball programs listed Gola as 6'7" tall. He was the tallest man on La Salle's team. (After graduation, the U.S. Army draft board measured him at a shade under 6'6" tall, making him eligible to be drafted into the army.) Gola was also the fastest man on the team, and had the quickest reflexes. Unlike most basketball teams that played their tallest man directly in front of the basket,

La Salle moved Tom Gola inside and out, making it difficult for opposing teams to defend against him.

One measure of the influence exerted by an outstanding athlete is the extent to which other players adopt his style of play. One of the first things about Gola that caught my attention was his complete lack of any facial expression during a game. Regardless of the effort that went into any move on the court, Tom's face remained expressionless. Sportswriters called him "phlegmatic." I looked up the word in the dictionary. *The Oxford Universal Dictionary* defines a phlegmatic temperament as being "cool; self-possessed." I can recall only one time that Gola showed emotion on a basketball court.

It happened in one of the few games that Tom Gola played at Penn's Palestra. (La Salle College played its home games at convention hall, at the small gym on the college campus and at the gym in the new Lincoln High School in Northeast Philadelphia.) In 1954, the Palestra was host to the eastern regionals of the NCAA Basketball Tournament. La Salle was matched against North Carolina State, led by Mel Thompson and Ron Shavlik. It was a close game, and State was turning up the pressure with an increasingly physical defense. Gola got a step on his defender, and drove down the lane for what looked like a sure goal when a well-placed forearm sent him sprawling across the court. The facial expression remained unchanged but you could see the fire in his eyes. He made both of the foul shots. On the next series, Gola helped La Salle break a full-court press by coming back to the mid-court line to take a pass. Hardly did the ball touch his hands, when Gola flipped a pass back over his head to the basket where teammate Bob Maples was waiting unguarded. Fans wondered how Gola knew Maples was there. Gola rebounded; he brought the ball up court; he set up plays; he scored; and La Salle won handily.

This was the end of the old two-handed set shot era. Gola rarely took a set shot, but when he did it was the one-hand variety. When it came to foul shots, basketball traditionalists still favored the two-hander. Many of them used the underhand two-handers that were a trademark of Bill Sharman of the Boston Celtics. Sharman rarely missed a foul shot. But Tom Gola shot a one-hander from the foul line, and most Philadelphia players followed suit.

Defensively, Gola used his long arms and quick hands to great advantage. He frequently blocked shots, but unlike other dominant defenders, he did not swat an opponent's shot into the stands. He caught the ball in flight and immediately threw it to one of his teammates on a fast break. Frank Selvy, a sharpshooter from Furman University in South Carolina, came to convention hall with the reputation for having scored 100 points in one game. Against La Salle, Selvy went right at Tom Gola with a running jump shot near the foul line. Gola's quick hands stole the ball cleanly, and his fast feet led to a layup at the other end of the court.

He seemed to glide the last few steps to the basket. Gola rarely dunked the ball. He laid it softly against the backboard and let it fall into the hoop.

Local basketball players copied Gola's signature defense against aggressive drives to the basket. He approached the opponent, almost daring him to extend the ball within reach. Usually, the opponent would move the ball back while driving forward. Gola then leaned around behind the player and flicked

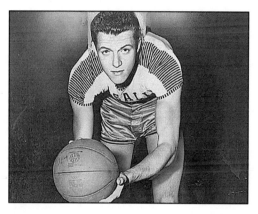

the ball away. Ten years later, Northeast Philadelphia's Jim Halpin introduced that move to his teammates at The Citadel in South Carolina. It is described by author Pat Conroy in his memoir *My Losing Season*. Conroy never forgot that defensive move but he did not realize that it was part of the legacy of Tom Gola.

Gola's legacy is impressive. He is a member of the Naismith Basketball Hall of Fame and the Philadelphia Big5 Hall of Fame. He was a 4-time All America selection, the Most Valuable Player of the 1952 NIT, the Most Outstanding player of the 1954 NCAA Basketball Tournament, and a 5-time NBA All-Star. His teams won the 1952 NIT, and the 1954 NCAA Tournaments, and finished second in the 1955 NCAA Tournament. In 1956, he led the Philadelphia Warriors to the NBA Championship. In 1968, when La Salle's basketball program hit the skids, Tom Gola returned to the campus and coached the basketball team to a second place finish in the national rankings. Significantly, his college awards were achieved with teams that were not stocked with blue-chip players. Coach Ken Loeffler put it this way, "My team was Tom Gola plus four students." Tom Gola made everyone around him a better player.

When his playing and coaching days were over, Gola won election as a representative in the Pennsylvania legislature, and then as City Controller of Philadelphia. In 1981, he was appointed regional administrator of the Department of Housing and Urban Development. In the meanwhile, he ran his own insurance business and dabbled in things like running a golf driving range.

Over the years, I had occasional contact with Tom Gola. He continued to play softball with his old friends at 50-50 Tavern in the Olney Tavern League. He still hit the ball a mile. In 1986, I met him briefly at a luncheon when he was inducted as a coach into the Big5 Basketball Hall of Fame. Tom never played in the Big5. It was started in 1955, three months after he graduated from college. Nonetheless, in 2000 the Philadelphia

Big5 held a special induction for a few old-timers who played their college ball in Philadelphia and should not be left out of any Philadelphia basketball hall of fame: Tom Gola, Paul Arizin, Ernie Beck, Bill Mlkvy and George Senesky.

They held the old-timers ceremony just in time. In the summer of 2003, Tom was leaving a suburban restaurant when he tripped, fell backward and struck his head on a curb. He lapsed into a coma and was hospitalized. Rumors circulated that Gola suffered a stroke, maybe multiple strokes. He spent time in a nursing home. He spent time in seclusion in Florida. He withdrew from the public eye.

I last saw Tom Gola five years ago at the inaugural of the Northeast Philadelphia Hall of Fame, held at Holy Family University. This award is not centered on athletics. It recognizes achievement and significant, positive impact on the community. Tom was one of the initial inductees. I left the pre-ceremony reception early so I could get a good seat for the presentation. As I reached the doorway to the theater, two men approached from my right. One man was assisting the other who was obviously disabled and struggling with a cane. The man with the cane was twisted and hunched forward. I grabbed the closest door and held it open for them. When they started down the aisle, I realized I had just held the door for a long-time hero.

Tom Gola was a public citizen. He personified Philadelphia in the last half of the twentieth century. He transformed individual talent into a symphony that captured the imagination of the entire country. When Tom passed away two weeks ago, sportswriters, most of whom are not old enough to have seen Tom Gola play, looked at his basketball statistics and declared that Gola "was an early version of Magic Johnson." It was a declaration that disparaged both men. Johnson was a good basketball player, but Magic Johnson is no Tom Gola.

The congregation at St. Albert the Great was a "Who's Who" of Philadelphia basketball, a gathering of La Salle alumni and sports fans in general. Prominent among the mourners were Charley Greenberg, a guard on the 1954 NCAA championship team, and Ernie Beck, the Penn All-America who played with Tom on the 1956 NBA champion Philadelphia Warriors. Wilt Chamberlain was wrong. Sometimes people do root for Goliath. This was a time for heroes.

Of course, Father Breen made it to the funeral. He was one of the concelebrants of the Mass. (Fr. Breen is in the back row, on the right in this photo.)

At the church they distributed a small memorial card with a photo of Tom taken about ten years ago. On the reverse side of the card was the following inscription:

"Today I am a contented person,
I gave it my best in all that I did,
in sports, businesses
and in public office.
I would have never
second-guessed myself."

Tom Gola

ROLLS' STORY

Last Wednesday, my high school class met for lunch at Normandy Farm. It was the week after Tom Gola's funeral, and much of our conversation centered on memories of Tom and his impact on both La Salle High School and La Salle College. Gola was a senior at the high school when we were freshmen. The following year, he led the college's basketball team to the championship of the National Invitation Tournament in New York City. In our senior year of high school, Tom led La Salle College to the championship of the NCAA Basketball Tournament. That was 1954, and it was a different world.

The national championship game was played in Kansas City, Missouri. It was the first NCAA championship game to be televised nationwide. The technology was primitive. The screen was small. The cameras were distant. And it looked as though they were playing in a snowstorm. But it was better than the alternative – a radio broadcast that depended on the language skills of the announcers and the imagination of the listeners. When the game ended, they announced that the La Salle team would fly back to Philadelphia the following night. That was a signal for many of La Salle's Philadelphia fans to be at the airport to meet the returning champions. One of those fans was Jim "Rolls" Trainer.

Rolls smiled at his memories of sixty years ago. He looked around at each of us and said that the return of La Salle's 1954 championship team had long been a source of personal angst. Rolls' father decided that the family would drive down to the airport and meet the team. Sunday evening they all piled into the Trainer family car and headed for the airport. In 1954, Philadelphia International Airport was a different place. The parking lot was much smaller, and it lacked any clear identification of parking locations. To remember where a car was parked, you had to line it up with some recognizable physical feature. There were no security checks. Anyone could walk out on the tarmac, right next to the arriving plane.

Rolls' brother David did just that; making sure that he stayed near Tom Gola when the official photos were taken.

64//Crushing the Competition

The Explorers solidified La Salle's place on the college basketball map with a crushing 92-76 victory over Bradley College to claim the 1954 NCAA championship. In the first nationally televised NCAA game, the Explorers became just the third Eastern team in history to win a national championship thanks to players such as Tom Gola, '55.

Dave's photo appeared on the front page of the Philadelphia newspapers the following day. It looked like he was a member of the team.

In the meanwhile, most of Rolls' friends decided that they were going back to the La Salle campus at 20th and Olney Avenue. Rolls decided to join them. Forgetting that he had come to the airport with his parents, he hopped into a friend's car. His brother Dave had the same idea. Dave jumped into another car. As the celebratory group wound its way to 20th and Olney, Rolls suddenly remembered his parents back at the airport – and that David had the car keys in his pocket. His parents were now isolated at Philadelphia International Airport without any means of getting home except for calling a cab – a very expensive cab. Rolls was embarrassed and guilt-stricken to have caused such grief to his parents. When he got home the next morning, he did not mention the subject of the car or his parents' cab ride home, preferring instead to let his parents raise the issue. No one said anything, so neither did Rolls. The subject was not mentioned in the Trainer household for years; and the years went by. On the other hand, hardly a day went by when Rolls did not berate himself for leaving his parents isolated at the airport in the middle of the night.

Last week, Rolls approached one of his sisters. "Agnes, you went with us to the airport to meet that La Salle championship team, didn't you?" She answered in the affirmative.

"Well how did you and mom and dad get home that night?"

"At the last minute, David remembered that he had the keys to the car. As he was going out the gate, he threw the keys out the window to my friend Mary Alice. She gave the keys to me, and I drove home. The only problem we had was finding the car in the parking lot."

And for the next sixty years, Rolls Trainer beat himself up daily because of an ancient wrong that existed only in his imagination. No good deed should go unpunished.

WOODLAND STEEL FABRICATORS

Woodland Steel Fabricators was located on Shackamaxon Street in Philadelphia. It was, for all intents and purposes, a two-man operation. Fred Woodland was the owner and the sole business-getter of the company. Woodland was a big man, fiftyish, with a thick head of gray hair. Austin Fenerty was the shop foreman. He was one of those rare people who loves to work. A slender man with a perpetual smile, Aus was never happier than when he was creating a product that, up to that time, was only a drawing on a set of blueprints. Together, Fred and Aus ran a successful small business, cutting, drilling, and shaping raw steel, so that it could be assembled into a finished product. In the summer of 1954, it occurred to Fred that the business would operate more efficiently if there was someone in the office to answer the phone while he was making sales calls and Aus was busy working in the shop. Fred mentioned this thought to my father, and the following week I began a three-month term as the office clerk for Woodland Steel Fabricators.

Shackamaxon was a "mixed use" street. It was a short walk from the Girard Avenue Elevated Station. Whereas Girard Avenue, with its two sets of trolley tracks and imposing continuity of commercial storefronts was clearly a big-city street, Shackamaxon Street was just a narrow civic appendage. On both sides of Shackamaxon Street were sporadic groups of private homes, situated side-by-side with manufacturing businesses. Beyond the far end of the block was Richmond Street where the refinery buildings of the infamous "Sugar Trust" were located. A block or so to the left on Delaware Avenue was Penn Treaty Park, where William Penn signed a treaty with the Indians back in the 1600s. The general area was called Fishtown, but the people who lived in these densely populated streets near Penn Treaty Park called their neighborhood "Shackamaxon," the name given to it by the Delaware Tribe who negotiated with William Penn long ago.

Woodland Steel Fabricators was located toward the Richmond Street end of the block, at about 1112-16 Shackamaxon Street. I have long since lost the exact address. Three granite block steps flanked by an iron railing led to the front door of the office. Immediately to the left of the office building was a driveway and a partially-open shed that extended all the way to the back of the property line. The shed was the fabricators' workshop. In earlier days, it was probably a livery stable. Directly across the street were four small houses occupied by young families. One of those families regularly put a baby carriage out on the sidewalk in front of the house. The infant seemed to have no trouble sleeping, even with the high-pitched whine of the metal saws coming from our shop.

Most days I was alone in the office. It was the plain kind of place that you would expect of a shop-office in the mid-1950s.

The heavy wooden furniture looked as though it might have been there when William Penn arrived in 1682. Fred Woodland's desk was in front of the double window. To the left of the desk was a long counter that served as my desk and also as a place to spread out blueprints for the company's jobs. On Fred's desk there was an old-fashioned black rotary phone and, on the table across the room, one of those oscillating GE fans that seemed to be universal in the days before air conditioning. Aus would come into the office on occasion, but usually he stuck to the shop. Fred almost always was out visiting customers or suppliers.

When he was in the office around noontime, Fred often asked me to walk a couple blocks to a neighborhood delicatessen to pick up a sandwich for him. Fred liked beerwurst on rye bread. For my part, I enjoyed the walk through the neighborhood. I would often change my route to the deli so that I could get to know the neighborhood better. The streets were narrow. The houses were small, but well maintained. On occasion, I would walk up to Penn Treaty Park and wonder what the area looked like three hundred years ago. I enjoyed talking to the owners of the deli. Shop owners can tell you a lot about a neighborhood.

Back at the office, Fred liked to engage in conversation. We talked about a lot of things: the steel fabricating business, the Shackamaxon neighborhood, Phillies baseball and how I spent my free time. Invariably, the subject of our conversations turned to his son. Fred Woodland's son was just a few years older than me.

Fred was convinced that his son made a big mistake in life – he got married shortly after graduating from high school. "He never experienced the fun and good times that most young people enjoy. He went from childhood directly to the heavy responsibilities of fatherhood, with a wife and children dependent on him. He missed that transitional phase that should be a part of growing up," complained Fred. I kept my mouth shut. I did not know Fred's son, or his circumstances. There are times when the best you can do is just listen. These were such times.

Fred's concern for his son emphasized the economic stress of providing support for one's family. Maybe Fred could sense economic change in the air of the steel fabrication business. For some businesses, the 1950s and 1960s were boom times with a robust economy and lots of money. For example, real estate and construction were experiencing record growth, spurred by government programs. Urban renewal was changing the face of downtown Philadelphia, moving the food distribution businesses out of the Dock Street area and down to the open fields of South Philadelphia, near the Navy Yard. Drab warehouse buildings were being torn down and historic colonial buildings were being restored and, in some cases, rebuilt. But, as is often the case in life, Newton's third law applied: for every action there is an equal but opposite reaction. In Philadelphia, that opposite reaction was called Interstate – 95.

Interstate – 95 is a highway that tore the heart and soul out of several Philadelphia neighborhoods; but none more than Shackamaxon. It cut a swath nearly 500-yards wide, right up the eastern boundary of the neighborhood, leaving barely enough room between the elevated highway and the Delaware River to squeeze in historic Penn Treaty Park. The highway also took out the houses where the delicatessen used to be. For those homeowners whose properties remained untouched by the condemnation process, it was like living under one of the runways at International Airport. When they filmed the movie "Rocky" and all of its progeny, they made sure that the cameras were pointed away from I–95. People could understand the Market-Frankford Elevated trains, but I-95 is a piece of life that is hard to swallow.

In the meanwhile, steel producers were being hit with tough competition from foreign firms. The industry was consolidating. U.S. Steel and Bethlehem Steel went out of business. Distributors and erectors competed for the business that was previously done by steel fabricators. Pretty soon, Woodland Steel Fabricators shut its doors; one more victim of progress. By that time, not only was the summer of 1954 behind me, but so too were my college days. It was a time of universal military service, and I was a part of that universe. I was a second lieutenant in the United States Marine Corps stationed at Marine Corps Schools, Quantico, Virginia.

49

My assignment at Marine Corps Schools was like flying in a holding pattern over the east coast. It would not last long. My contemporaries and I owed substantial amounts of money to the Bank of Quantico which financed our purchases of full sets of summer and winter uniforms and the usual accompaniments such as swords and swagger sticks. (Swagger sticks soon went the fateful way of steel fabricators.) As soon as The Basic School ended, we could expect to receive orders to new duty stations, which in my case turned out to be Camp Pendleton, California and Camp Schwab, Okinawa. With those moves would come new responsibilities and new financial pressures. Throughout this time, I could plainly hear Fred Woodland's warnings about too much, too soon. Those Shackamaxon conversations followed me across the country and over the Pacific Ocean. In many respects, Shackamaxon continues to follow me today, nearly sixty years after the fact.

When I am in the neighborhood, I drive down Shackamaxon Street and then continue down some of the small residential streets that managed to survive the interstate. More often, I will take a digital tour, compliments of Google maps. The computer gives you a unique view of the old neighborhood. Many things on the street have not changed. The four small houses across from Woodland's shop are still there. Of course, the baby carriage is no longer there. Its occupant is probably registering for Medicare. Woodland's property is still there, although its face has been changed. Some properties, here and there, have been demolished. Some were rebuilt; some were abandoned. The street and the buildings look like they could use a good scrubbing.

In contrast to my somewhat pessimistic view of the state of the street, the Internet contains a sales listing for the residential property at 1132-34 Shackamaxon Street. The property is described as "inconspicuous and unassuming." The asking price is just $1.1 million, which is neither inconspicuous nor unassuming. I am glad that someone on Shackamaxon Street made it to the big time.

ED MOORE

We grew up a few blocks from each other – you lived just beyond Rhawn Street; I lived on Chippendale Avenue. It was just a short distance but those few blocks made a big difference. They put you in St. Dominic's Parish and me in St. Matt's. We did not meet until our sophomore year at St. Joseph's College. We were in the same class for the Air Force ROTC program.

I can still picture you making an erudite presentation of a history of the World War I flying squadron known as "the Lafayette Escadrille." You should have told me that you lived in St. Dominic's Parish. Had I known that, I might not have pulled the rug out from under you by telling the class that the story came straight out of a recent edition of "Classic Comics." Hardly were the words out of my mouth when I realized my mistake in judgment. I wished that I could have called back those words. But what was done was done. You never forgot it. Over the next sixty years, every time we met, you would say, "Why did you do that?"

We both practiced law in Philadelphia for nearly fifty years but, like St. Dominic's and St. Matt's, we rarely came into contact with each other. That changed when you persuaded me to become involved with you in the Lower Dublin Academy, the Nazareth Academy Grade School, and the Historical Society of Frankford. One of a lawyer's duties is to act as a public citizen in furthering the goals of society. You certainly met that duty in exemplary fashion.

GRADUATION DAY

Perhaps the most memorable part of my graduation ceremony from La Salle High School in June 1954 was the attendance of Connie Mack, *nee* Cornelius McGillicuddy. Even at age 91, you could tell that in his day he had been a great athlete. At six feet four inches, he was taller than everyone in my graduating class except Gerry Griffin. He wore an old-fashioned celluloid collar and a straw skimmer hat, an outfit that immediately identified him as the owner and manager of the Philadelphia Athletics Baseball Club. Unlike most managers in professional baseball, he saw no reason to try to look like a ballplayer when he was managing. He looked for all the world like an undertaker sitting at the far end of the dugout near third base.

Connie Mack was a legend in his own time. Nearly everyone at the graduation was turning to get a good look at him. Until that day, I had no idea that Connie Mack was Frank Cunningham's grandfather.

Remembering JFK

Here I am, nearly twenty-seven years of age, sitting in the gutter of a street about one block from the White House. It is 8:30 A.M. on a cold November morning in 1963. No, this is not a down-and-out story. There were thousands of people lining the streets that morning. Estimates ran as high as one million persons. We were there for the funeral of President John Fitzgerald Kennedy.

It was a spur-of-the-moment decision, made shortly after midnight on a Sunday evening. I was accustomed to the long drive to Washington, D.C. Three years earlier it was part of my regular route to and from the Marine Corps Base in Quantico, Virginia. At that time, Route 40 was the principal highway. Now – just eleven days ago – President Kennedy opened the new interstate highway between Wilmington, Delaware and Baltimore, Maryland. We could access that new interstate at Chester, Pennsylvania. Although the route was officially designated Interstate-95, state leaders in Maryland and Delaware were already talking about naming the highway in memory of President Kennedy. Driving on the limited access road was much easier than navigating the old Route 40, with its 120-mile string of traffic lights. Still, it was a long, dark drive. Dawn was breaking when we arrived at the Capitol grounds. Our first job was to find a parking space. Thanks to our 7:00 A.M. arrival time, parking was not a problem.

The radio announced that the funeral cortege would leave

the Capitol Building at 8:30 A.M. Members of the public would be admitted to the rotunda until that time. We walked up to the Capitol. A line of people stretched out of the rotunda, down the steps, and across the plaza – and the line was getting longer by the minute. If we waited in that line, there was little chance that we would reach  the rotunda by 8:30. Instead, we decided to stake out an observation point on the route of the procession to the Cathedral. The only problem with that plan was that we didn't know where the Cathedral was located, or what route the procession would take.

There were hundreds of people milling around: tourists like us, and policemen and members of the military who were assisting with security. Everyone was helpful. We were told that the funeral procession would start at the White House and proceed north on 17th Street about four blocks to Connecticut Avenue, and then another block to St. Matthew's Cathedral. It was about a two-mile walk from the Capitol to 17th Street. We were among the first persons to take a vantage point at that location. Gradually, additional observers arrived and the site became quite crowded. The growing crowd ebbed and flowed like a tide. Pretty soon there were several people in front of me. Unless I was satisfied with photos of the backs of their heads, something had to be done to improve my vista. That was when I decided to take my place in the gutter.

I was concerned that the police and the secret service might tell me to put away my camera for fear that the small metallic object might be a pistol. Several policemen approached me but apparently I looked harmless; they walked away without saying anything. Then, a disturbing thought struck me. I did not know what to expect in the way of a funeral procession. It was just the third day after President Kennedy was murdered. Confusion reigned. Federal agents and Dallas police officials openly clashed over who was in control of the crime scene. The Dallas coroner ordered that Kennedy's body not be removed from Dallas until an autopsy was conducted. Kennedy's people disregarded that order. There was a great deal of speculation about the funeral. Only yesterday was it announced that the funeral Mass would be celebrated at St. Matthew's Cathedral and the burial would be at Arlington National Cemetery. There had not been much time to make elaborate arrangements. I expected that there would be a few military units on parade, but now I began to worry it might be just a line of black limousines with dark-tinted windows racing up the street to the Cathedral. That would hardly be memorable.

We heard it long before we saw anything: the tattoo of muffled drums in the distance, the plaintive wail of bagpipes, the creaking of wooden wagon wheels, their metal rims crushing the stony street, and the clackety-clack-clack of steel horseshoes striking cobblestones. The sidewalks of 17th Street were jammed with people. It was a human canyon. Down that canyon came a swirl of color: the traditional red uniforms of the United States Marine Corps Band, "the President's Own," a 9-man contingent from Scotland's Black Watch wearing green tunics and red tartan kilts with large, shaggy black bearskin headdress.

By 1963, most of the cobblestones on Seventeenth Street had been paved over with macadam. But the macadam did not cover the cobblestones in the center of the street where they served as a bed for trolley tracks. Down this cobblestone path came a flag-draped caisson, pulled by six white horses accompanied by a sergeant on horseback. With every step, steel horseshoes clattered sharply against the hard stones. Adding to the cacophony of hoof beats was a prancing quarter-horse named Black Jack, his saddle empty and two boots reversed in the stirrups. He was an equine tap-dancer, and the cobblestones were his stage.

 Behind Black Jack walked Jacqueline Kennedy, dressed in black and flanked by the president's two brothers. Behind the Kennedys marched Lyndon and Lady Bird Johnson, and then many of the world's leaders. Charles de Gaulle, of France, and Haile Selassie, Emperor of Ethiopia, stood out in the crowd. De Gaulle was the tallest in the group, and Selassie, although the smallest, was resplendent in his black and gold braided uniform. There were officials from all branches of government, including the members of the Supreme Court of the United States. At both sides of each row of dignitaries were two or three security personnel, each looking to the back of the crowd and overhead to the windows and roofs of nearby buildings.

And yes, the military services were there. Soldiers, sailors, Coast Guard, Marines, Air Force, Special Forces, women's units, the military academies, bands and choirs were all in attendance. There was constant movement; and the creak of the caisson and the clatter of the horseshoes continued to resound up and down the length of that lonely street. It took about thirty minutes for the entire procession to pass by our location. At that point, I pulled myself out of the gutter and we began our two-mile trek back to the place where we parked the car.

It was a quiet ride home. Nonetheless, we were glad that we made the effort to attend JFK's final ceremony.

However difficult it may be to paint a word picture that captures the intensity of emotion that gripped our country in 1963, I remember it. I can still see it clearly; I can still hear it. Dominating that memory is the sound of prancing steel horseshoes on the cobblestones, set against the creak and crunch of wooden wagon wheels and the clatter of the draught horses. I'll never forget that sound.

Sights and sounds are easy to remember; less so the unspoken thoughts that occur during the course of an historic event. Hardly had we reached our vantage point on 17th Street

when my thoughts wandered back to a time in April 1945 – I was then eight years old. My father told me to get into the car, and he drove to 6th & Sedgley Avenue, where the overpass provided an excellent view of the railroad tracks below. Along with about one hundred other people, we watched a funeral train as it carried the body of President Franklin Delano Roosevelt north to his grave in Hyde Park, New York. At the time, I wondered whether there was some required ritual for those of us who watched the funeral train pass by. Some people waived; others saluted. Dad said that he just wanted to be there out of respect for the commander-in-chief whom he so greatly admired. I felt the same way about JFK. As the caisson rolled by, I half whispered, "Kennedy, I am here."

SHACKAMAXON

Small houses and small streets
At sharp angles to the wide river,
Where families and businesses grow and die
Side by side in the congested city.

In a coach by the front of the house,
An infant lies fast asleep;
While across the narrow street
Raw steel sings as steel-men ply their trade.

Beerwurst, a deli special,
Finds favor with the metalworkers.
The tiny street is hushed
When the metal shop closes.

The shop no longer sings.
Its customers are gone.
The small houses and the deli too,
Victims of progress all.

FRED EISELE

Sometimes you just don't want to know. Fred and I grew up together more than 65 years ago; he lived on the next block in northeast Philadelphia.

As a youngster, Fred was long and slender. He had the strongest throwing arm in the neighborhood. On the other hand, his ability to control the flight of the ball left something to be desired. Many a time I would emerge from our batting practice sessions tattooed by the baseballs that I could not dodge.

When Fred graduated from Lincoln High School, he had a good job waiting for him at The Budd Company, where his father worked as a tool and die maker. That was when Fred bought a well-used light blue 1949 Plymouth convertible. It came with several lengths of clothesline that we used to tie the doors shut. The car expanded our horizons for local sporting events, including the indoor basketball league at boathouse row on the Schuylkill River and our weekly jaunts to Jardel Recreation Center where we first saw Wilt Chamberlain play basketball.

I can still recall a drive to the home of the commanding officer of Fred's army reserve unit. He needed Fred's signature on the completed enlistment papers. However, when we arrived at the captain's home, I was the focus of his attention – not Fred. His main point was that if I signed up immediately, I would be eligible for the Korean War version of the G.I. Bill. It was a very persuasive recruiting pitch, but somehow I resisted the temptation.

Over the next year or two, Fred continued to work on his basketball game, particularly his long-range jump shot. He kept improving. Then, working through one of the coaches at Lincoln High, he was offered a scholarship to Penn State. That ended his career as a tool and die maker.

About ten years ago, we reestablished contact by e-mail over the Internet. We swapped many stories and nostalgic memories of our days on Oakmont and Chippendale Streets in northeast Philadelphia. We also shared prayers for ourselves, our friends and our families. Fred's last message came three months ago. I knew something was wrong, but I didn't want to know that my suspicions were true.

ZOUNDS OF YESTERYEAR

Zounds!

Some of you will remember that as a word from comic books. But, it sounds like "sounds" and not too many zounds have been emanating from my computer lately.

"Yesteryear" is another neat word from the past. Remember? "Come back with us now to those thrilling days of yesteryear!" And then, "From out of the past come the thundering hoofbeats of the great horse Silver. The Lone Ranger rides again!" I still find myself checking my watch at 7:30 p.m. on Mondays, Wednesdays and Fridays. Old habits die hard.

Zounds of bagpipes bring back images of an ancient parade eastward on Cottman Avenue and then turning north at Rowland Avenue. We were standing on the sidewalk by Fluehr's Funeral Home. The pipers stopped right in front of us. It must have been summertime because they were sweating, and glancing furtively at Schmidt's Tavern on the far side of the street. It was hard to imagine anyone sweating while playing a bagpipe.

FRANK REED

We enjoyed our time at Saint Joseph's College back in the 1950s. You particularly liked the publicity you got when I put your name in the "Czar's Column" in the school newspaper. After college, we both went into the Marine Corps; but you took a shortcut. You got out quick. Do you remember when we showed up at Jim Morris' wedding in uniform, complete with swagger sticks? Jim liked that.

There was Ocean City, Sea Isle, Margate and LeRoy Bostic at the Princeton Hotel in Avalon. People thought we were kidding that Sunday evening when we left Drexelbrook and drove down to Washington, D.C. to attend the funeral of President Kennedy in the morning. Back in those days we also met on Monday evenings at the Shrine in Germantown. Do you think people still go to the Shrine?

After embarking on the sea of matrimony, our get-togethers were less frequent. In recent years, it was mainly at the annual fund-raisers for the Marine Corps scholarship program. On the other hand, we did communicate by e-mail. Just three weeks ago we exchanged memories of our weekends at Bock's Pocono Trail Lodge. We remember the good times – and the good people.

CHINK'S STEAKS

This morning's *Philadelphia Inquirer* headline trumpets a story about the neighborhood steak sandwich place that changed  its name from "Chink's" to "Joe's," after doing business at the same Wissinoming location for 64 years. The sandwich shop was named for its original owner, Samuel "Chink" Sherman. Recently, the name came under attack by some members of Philadelphia's Asian-American community who consider the name "Chink" to be an offensive slur against people from Asia. If a slur it be, it was not always that. Back in the 1950s, "Chink" was a fairly common nickname. West Philadelphia High's Ray "Chink" Scott was one of the best basketball players ever to come out of Philadelphia. No one complained about Chink Scott's nickname – not even Wilt Chamberlain who challenged Scott for "bragging rights" on West Philadelphia's basketball courts.

The current media frenzy over the name "Chink" reminds me of an experience that I had in the early-1970s. I was a lawyer representing Yellow Cab Company of Philadelphia in the defense of a personal injury claim brought on behalf of a youngster who suffered a broken leg when he tried to run across a busy street in his densely populated neighborhood. (A "child dart-out case" was the way that the cab company described it.) An arbitration panel of three lawyers held the cab driver liable for the accident, and entered an award in favor of the young plaintiff. I filed an appeal on behalf of the cab company in the Court of Common Pleas of Philadelphia. Filing such appeals was a fairly common procedure, particularly for Yellow Cab. The appeal resulted in a new trial before a judge and jury. Who knows? The jury might see things differently from the three-lawyer arbitration panel. So too might the trial judge. Those were my hopes before I learned that the appeal was assigned to Judge Raymond Pace Alexander.

In those days, Raymond Pace Alexander was regarded as the dean of African-American judges in Philadelphia. A graduate of the University of Pennsylvania's Wharton School, and Harvard Law School, his slender, dignified appearance was immediately recognizable in the legal community. Even with his stellar academic background and more than forty years experience as a Philadelphia lawyer, it was difficult for him to get the bar association's recommendation to serve as a judge. However, after a full investigation, the nomination was approved; he was elected and had served on the bench for more than ten years by the time my case came up on appeal. Clearly, Judge Alexander was not likely to give preferential treatment to Yellow Cab Company and against an injured neighborhood child in a case that three experienced lawyers had already determined was the fault of the cab company.

 To make matters worse, the plaintiff was represented by Hardy Williams, a very likable lawyer, a Korean War veteran, who looked like he was still in good enough shape to play basketball for his West Philadelphia High School alma mater. Williams played for West Philadelphia about ten years before Chink Scott. Hardy was a recognized leader of the African-American community in Philadelphia politics. At the time of our pretrial conference, his political star was in the ascendant. You didn't have to be a genius to know that I did not stand a chance in this appeal.

Judge Alexander began the conference by inviting Hardy Williams to state the facts of the accident. Hardy had barely begun when the judge interrupted in an awkward manner. "This boy — the plaintiff — is he . . . Oh how do I say it? — of color?" Before Hardy could respond, the judge went on to explain his hesitation. "All my life, I have been involved in civil rights work. An important part of that work has been to protest the use of disparaging terms, and to avoid my own inadvertent misuse of that disparagement. We worked long and hard to eliminate the use of the word 'Nigger.' Gradually, we settled on two acceptable words, 'negro' and 'colored.' Now, people are beginning to take offense at those words, calling them 'patronizing' – and I just cannot bring myself to use the word 'Black.' We have always considered that word to be an insult. But that is the word that people seem to want nowadays." Hardy interrupted the soliloquy, and said, "Yes Judge, he is one of us." Insofar as the claim against Yellow Cab Company was concerned, it did not matter whether the young plaintiff was black or white — or green for that matter. There was no way that the cab company could prevail in that courtroom. I would see to it that the case was settled quickly. It was also a case that would be quickly forgotten. On the other hand, it will be a long time before I forget Judge Raymond Pace Alexander and his thoughts on the use of words of disparagement.

It seems that a cottage industry has recently emerged to find disparagement in commonly used words and images. In my childhood years, we used to identify with many members of the American Indian tribes, including chiefs like Geronimo, Sitting Bull, Prince Joseph, and of course the Lone Ranger's faithful companion Tonto. In recent years, that has changed. The public news media now tells us that identification with American Indians is exploitative and should be stopped. About twenty years ago, St. John's University in New York changed its nickname from the "Redmen" to the "Red Storm." The Atlanta Braves baseball team dropped its "screaming Indian" logo from its batting practice caps, and even considered eliminating its traditional chant known as the "Tomahawk Chop." Similarly, the Cleveland Indians and the Washington Redskins football club survived challenges to their long-standing identities.

The editorial board of the *Philadelphia Inquirer* sprung to the defense of its journalists, declaring that the name Chink's "required a certain heedlessness of the very existence of Asian Americans." Nothing was said about being heedless of common sense, or ignoring the intent and meaning of the words used. I wonder what Raymond Pace Alexander and Hardy Williams would have thought of "Chink's Steaks." Not much, I'll bet. Neither Judge Alexander nor Hardy Williams went out of his way to create disparagement where none exists. They focused their efforts on real insults, and finding ways to resolve them.

COHAN ON CONTRACTS

Not long after I graduated from law school, I was walking north on 15th Street toward City Hall, when I saw Leo Carlin's father at the far end of the block walking in my direction. I recognized him immediately. He was short and slender, and walked like a 70-year old bantam rooster. I was not sure that he would recognize me. He was the dean of the theater ticket business in Philadelphia, and he had short-term contact with hundreds of people every day. He could not possibly remember every person he met; much less remember all of the friends of his five children. I kept him in the corner of my eye so that I would be ready to wave if he did happen to recognize me. There was no sign of recognition – until we were about fifteen feet apart.

At that point, Mr. Carlin reacted like a World War II fighter plane. His head (and the little straw hat on top of it) dipped to the left, then his shoulder dipped to the left and his feet pivoted sharply in my direction. He stopped right in front of me. Waving his hand in my face, he said,

"When George M. Cohan came to town, we had an agreement how his shows would be handled. It was a 'handshake' agreement. Each of us knew what that meant, and we never had a problem. Then, Cohan dropped out of the theater business for several years. When he came back, he said, 'Lex, we'll handle the shows the same way that we always did; with the same handshake.' I said, 'No George, times have changed. We must have a written contract.' George M. Cohan looked at me and said, 'Contracts are for thieves *and lawyers!*'"

Without another word, Mr. Carlin pivoted to my left and continued his strut down 15th Street.

A SNAPSHOT IN TIME

No, it is not a great photo. There is no sense of movement, much less speed, balance, or grace. The ball is nowhere to be seen. All eyes are up, probably looking for the ball. It is as if the players are sneaking an extra breath of air while everyone is looking at the backboard. But wait! There on the left

edge of the photo, next to Jack Egan's hip, see the fellow dressed in a coat and tie, and wearing horn-rimmed glasses? That's me. This is the only known photograph of the best seat that I ever had for an NCAA basketball tournament game.

It all started on Wednesday, March 11, 1959. I was in charge of the intramural sports program at St. Joseph's College, and I spent a good bit of time in the fieldhouse. That particular afternoon I wanted to make sure that all of the scheduled basketball games were completed. St. Joe's was a small school. There were only three courts available on which to play all of the intramural league games. It was a particularly busy time that month what with the varsity basketball team having been selected to participate in the eastern regionals of the NCAA tournament. St. Joe's was scheduled to play against top-rated West Virginia and its superstar Jerry West, in Charlotte, North Carolina, on Friday night.

I was a St. Joe basketball fanatic. I would have loved to go to that game but I was financially challenged. I could handle the price of the tickets; and I could go on a starvation diet for three days; but the cost of travel and a motel room were beyond my meager resources. Maybe it was a good thing that the issue was cut and dried. A lot of my friends were in the same boat. We would not mope around feeling sorry for ourselves. I had just finished an intramural game and was resting at the end of the court, when I noticed a silhouetted figure waving at me from the main entrance of the gym.

It was Ray Adamczyk. He graduated in 1956, in what I thought of as, "Mike Fallon's class." Ray probably did not know anyone else in the gym. He looked relieved when I acknowledged his wave and walked over to him. He asked about the availability of tickets for the tournament games. I had no official position in the ticket office, but I regularly helped out with the sale of tickets and other athletic department chores. I was able to direct Ray to the office where he had no difficulty purchasing tickets for the games. As we talked, he said that he remembered what it is like to be a student, and that he and his fiancé would be glad to give a ride to any students who were going to the games this weekend.

"Just tell them to meet me here tomorrow at 5:30 p.m." At about that time, Jim Gavaghan joined us and said, "I'm going!" When Don McBride heard about our plans, he made it a threesome. We did not know where we were going to sleep, but we were going south, "y'all."

On Thursday evening, the three of us met Ray and his fiancé at the fieldhouse and began our journey. I had no idea how long it would take to drive to Charlotte. I assumed that we had plenty of time because we were starting out more than twenty-four hours before game time. I would learn. Our differences in outlook soon became apparent. Ray and his fiancé had their reservations in Charlotte. It was okay with them if we arrived in Charlotte 30 minutes before game time. On the other hand, Don, Gav and I needed time to scrounge places to stay after the game. We wanted to get to Charlotte as quickly as possible, but it was not our decision to make. It was Ray's car. Ray stayed well below the speed limit on every highway, regardless of the volume of traffic. Keep in mind that this was before the days of the interstate highway system. The speed limits were designed for horse and buggy traffic. We plodded down Route 15, past Gettysburg and by the civil war battlefields at about the same speed that Robert E. Lee had traveled a century before.

Gav offered and re-offered to share the driving chores. Finally, Ray relented and let Gav assume the driving. Don and I moved up to the front seat; we let Ray and his fiancé have exclusive possession of the back seat (which would also make it difficult for them to see the speedometer). It was nearly midnight when we wound our way through the town of Culpeper. Through the early morning hours, Gav's driving made a big difference in the distance that we covered. Shortly before daybreak, Ray awakened and said that he would resume the driving chores. As expected, our progress slowed noticeably. However, we pushed on at Ray's unperturbed pace until finally we pulled up to the Charlotte Carousel sports complex and the sprawling Carousel Motel. It was nearly 11:00 a.m. We made arrangements to meet Ray after the second game on Saturday night, and then set out to find someone who might let us spend the night in their room.

The Carousel Motel was like a college town. All four teams and most of their supporters were staying there. It was not long before Gav ran into some members of the track team who agreed to let him stay in their motel room. One down and two to go. We saw plenty of people that we knew, but getting a place to stay was something else. We were walking by the area occupied by the U.S. Naval Academy basketball team when someone called out Don McBride's name. It was Fran Delano, who had been a high school classmate of Don's at St. Joe's Prep in Philadelphia. Fran was a member of the Naval Academy team. He spoke to his roommate Ron Doyle, and they said that Don and I were welcome to stay in their room. "Just stay out of the way of Coach Carnevale." Later, Doyle made arrangements to move in with another teammate who had a room by himself.

84

Things were working out very well. We had our tickets to the game. We bought them before we left St. Joseph's, but we had no idea where they were located. The tickets said "Row DDDD." That meant nothing to us. The meaning became crystal clear when we showed the tickets to the usher at the base of the Carousel stairway. He pointed up — way, way up. I began to feel dizzy. In a minor state of panic, my eyes raced around the arena. Down at courtside was a long table that ran along the edge of the basketball court. There were seats for the official scorer, the timekeeper, radio sportscasters and newspaper reporters. Significantly, at the right end of the table there were three empty seats . . . three empty seats. Now, I wasn't born yesterday. I knew that those seats were reserved for somebody important. We were not important. Undoubtedly, any approach to those seats would be quickly and publicly rebuffed. Why bother? I looked again at our tickets – and I looked up at Row DDDD – and whispered to Don and Gav, "Pull out a piece of paper and a pencil; we'll tell them that we are reporters for the college newspaper."

I was surprised that we made it all the way to the table. Once there, we hunkered down and pretended to make notes on the scraps of paper that we tore from the official program. I kept waiting for the sword to drop. It never happened. Midway through the first half, I began to relax and enjoy the game. Don McBride was sitting to my left. To Don's left was the radio broadcasting crew. Between them was a telephone. It was 1959, the era of The Bell System and AT&T Long Lines. Long distance phone calls were a big deal. Don picked up the phone and dialed his home number. His family was listening to the game on the radio. They could not believe that Don was calling from courtside. The following night we came back, and the seats were still there. This time we had no hesitation. We felt that we were entitled to those seats.

And what about the games? They did not go as well as we hoped. St. Joe started off against West Virginia like a house afire. The Hawks had an 18-point lead midway through the second half. Then West Virginia began a pressure defense and the referees began to call a one-sided stream of personal fouls against St. Joe's, usually offensive fouls. There were 32 personal fouls called against St. Joseph's as opposed to only 20 against West Virginia. Four of St. Joseph's five starting players and their first substitute off the bench fouled out of the game. Joe Gallo, the fifth starter, was on the verge of fouling out with four fouls called against him. None of the West Virginia players fouled out of the game. Jerry West was spectacular, scoring 36 points to lead West Virginia to a 95-92 victory. In the consolation game on Saturday night, Navy beat a disheartened St. Joe's team 70-56.

When classes resumed the following week, Bernie Scally asked me to draft a letter from him as president of the Student Council of St. Joseph's College to the NCAA, complaining about the one-sided officiating in the West Virginia game. I told Bernie that I could not do that. I did not like what the referees had done, but the game was over, and it was time to move on. We did move on, but some small part of that distant weekend in Charlotte has lingered in me.

In the fall of 1959, I frequently found myself driving through Culpeper, Virginia, and the civil war battlefields to and from my first active duty assignment at Marine Corps Base, Quantico, Virginia. Culpeper always reminds me of that long drive to Charlotte. While attending The Officers Basic School in Quantico, we were joined by a class of freshly minted second lieutenants from the Naval Academy. Nearly all of them had been at the NCAA tournament and stayed at the Carousel Motel. They remembered it as a party weekend. Twenty-five years later I was reminded of Ron Retton, an unheralded substitute on the 1959 West Virginia team, when his daughter Mary Lou won a gold medal in gymnastics in the 1984 Olympics. That gave me an additional reason to root for Mary Lou.

Most of all, I find myself thinking of three courtside seats at the officials table. Things like that do not just "happen." Someone must have stepped back and let three college kids have their dream weekend. I don't know who was responsible, but this lucky beneficiary has been forever grateful. I am also glad that this experience was preserved in an almost forgotten black-and-white photograph in the St. Joseph's University archives. Go Hawks!

The Senior Mile

The current issue of *First Things*, the publication of the Institute on Religion and Public Life, has an interesting note about a Spanish long-distance runner named Iván Fernández Anaya. He was participating in a cross-country meet on the outskirts of Pamplona, and was well behind the leader, an internationally known runner from Kenya. Suddenly, the Kenyan came to a stop ten yards short of the finish line. He mistakenly thought that he had crossed the finish line and completed the race. Anaya had only to maintain his stride for a few more seconds and he would have breezed by the confused Kenyan and won the event; but he did not do that. Instead, Anaya pulled up behind the Kenyan and, using hand and arm signals, directed the Kenyan across the finish line. Anaya finished in second place. His coach was critical of his pupil's magnanimous action. While giving Anaya credit in human terms, the coach said that, "Winning always makes you more of an athlete. You have to go out to win." The *First Things* commentator was squarely in the other camp, concluding, "Three cheers, no, five cheers, *ten cheers*, for Iván Fernández Anaya."

For me, Iván Fernández Anaya brought back memories of a distant era. In October 1958, I was beginning my senior year at St. Joseph's College, in Philadelphia. It was a busy time. In addition to the academic regimen, I was in charge of the intramural sports program, writing a regular column for *The Hawk*, the college newspaper, and playing fullback for the new varsity soccer team. October brought an added demand in the form of a notice from my local draft board to report for induction into the army. I fooled them; I enlisted in the Marine Corps. In any event, my connection with athletics at the college made it inevitable that I would play some part in the traditional "Senior Mile."

I do not know how the Senior Mile came to be a tradition. In college, traditions come easy. "They did it last year . . . and maybe, the year before that." Suffice it to say, the Senior Mile was something like the Senior Prom. It was under the control of the student government, not the athletic department. Our class representatives selected the date, the time, the master of ceremonies, the judge – and even the queen of the event, Madeline Conti, secretary to Dean Matthew G. Sullivan, SJ. Joe McGinn was designated as the judge. My part was to arrange for an "Olympic flame" at the start of the event. Jim Gavaghan was a willing co-conspirator in that effort. Our plan was simple. We appropriated an old galvanized metal trash can, and we inverted the top so that it would form a basin for a small pool of gasoline. The can and the gasoline were placed in the first row of the old concrete grandstand that ran along the southeast side of the track, adjacent to Overbrook Avenue. The Olympic torch was made by wrapping an old shirt around one end of a four-foot piece of wood, and then securing the cloth tightly with wire so that it would not fall apart after the torch was lighted. It worked perfectly. Gav carried the lighted torch for one lap around the quarter-mile track, and then used the torch to ignite the pool of gasoline in the top of the trash can. We had our Olympic flame.

About a dozen students showed up to compete in the race. They seemed to be impressed by the pyrotechnics, and by the Ford Thunderbird convertible that George Weir used to chauffeur Mad Conti to the track. Aus Hogan, the class wit, made a few funny remarks, and Joe McGinn fired the starter's pistol, which sent the runners scurrying around the track for their four-lap race. After the first lap, a few of the runners dropped out of the race. Not long afterward, we heard a low, rumbling noise behind us. We turned around, and there the wind was blowing our Olympic flame across the first eight rows of seats. The concrete was indestructible, but the wooden benches were

beginning to catch fire. We had not planned for this contingency. We didn't even think to bring marshmallows. Finally, Gavaghan took charge. Taking advantage of a lull in the wind, he put his foot against the side of the trash can and nudged it – and its contents – over the front of the grandstand and onto the cinder track. There was one final giant flash as the pool of gasoline flared out in the wind. A few buckets of water took care of the smoldering benches.

Meanwhile, the race continued and only two seniors survived: Al McCart and Charlie Dougherty. It was a close race. As they came around the last turn, McCart was in the lead and was opening the gap. We stood at the south edge of the grandstand, cheering them on. Suddenly, Al McCart stopped running, about twenty yards short of the finish line. He thought that the group of spectators marked the finish line. Charlie Dougherty knew exactly where the finish line was, and he was running for it with all his strength. That was when Al McCart realized what happened, and he sprinted the last twenty yards, barely catching Charlie. Joe McGinn, our Solomon-like judge, ruled that the race was a tie. And so it was that the Class of 1959 Senior Mile was shared by Dougherty and McCart. Fortunately for some of us, the grandstand was demolished about a month later to make way for a new classroom building. No one mentioned the burned-out benches. We dodged a bullet.

On the other hand, there was plenty of talk about the exciting finish of the Senior Mile. Despite all of that talk, no one – absolutely no one – even suggested that Charlie Dougherty should have stopped running just because Al McCart made a mistake. We never gave it a thought. We weren't that smart. Three cheers? Five cheers? Ten cheers? We cheered the both of them, thanks to the ruling that the race ended in a tie. Good call, Joe!

George Pentram

Eddie Feigner used to complain about the irony of being a supremely talented athlete in the "peanut" sport of softball, a sport that no one cares about. You must have felt the same way

When you were pitching, the monotony was unbearable. I would stand near second base watching that tight figure-eight windup, and marvel at how the ball exploded from your left hand. The next pitch would be exactly the same, and the next one, and the next one and the next – nine consecutive pitches and it would be our turn at bat.

There were only about three players in the entire league who could get a bat on your fastball. And God help any fielder who was daydreaming and misplayed one of those infrequent hits. George, you had a way with words!

We were together on that Warnock Tavern team for only one season – and that was fifty years ago. But I will never forget the experience. Thanks for the memories.

CHRIS ANDREASEN

The steel frame double bunk in the middle of the second platoon's squadbay was one rugged piece of equipment. The bunk was used by the two biggest guys in the platoon, Ed Anderson and Chris Andreasen. It is hard to imagine the stresses applied to that steel frame by those two behemoths. But their size was not necessarily an advantage when it came to the hill trail.

It was about a month into the officer candidates program when the platoon was slated to cover the hill trail at a forced march pace. There was a strong implication that those candidates who could not handle the forced march would likely be dropped from the program. We knew the challenges of the hill trail. Basically, it was one and one-half miles across three ridgelines and into an open meadow. We used it regularly as the area where our training exercises took place. I was lucky. I was in great physical shape for the only time in my life, thanks to a tough college soccer program. For me, the hill trail was a piece of cake. On the other hand, I hated to be hemmed in by the close formation of our platoon. I enjoyed being on my own. Typically, I would slide out of the formation and run by myself behind the platoon, helping anyone who fell behind.

The beginning of the hill trail was deceptively simple. It was a winding path on level ground. Then, the path swung to the right and went uphill at a steep slope. Invariably, the pace slowed down and some people began to fall behind the main body. Ed Anderson and Chris Andreasen were among those who were dropping back toward my tail-end position.

As we clambered up the second hill, I came up beside Chris. Ed Anderson was just to our right. "C'mon, keep moving," I said. "I'm exhausted," Chris replied, "I can't make it." I pointed to a tree near the crest of the hill, and said, "See that tree; you can make it that far." Chris nodded his head in the affirmative. When we reached the tree, I told Chris that he certainly could make it to the top of the hill. Chris grunted and then chugged up to the top of the hill. "That's it!" he said, "That's as far as I can go." Ed Anderson signaled his agreement.

"Chris," I pleaded, "no one quits at the top of a hill! Anyone can go downhill, even if they are exhausted." That made sense. So, we chugged down the other side of the hill. Near the bottom, I suggested, "Let's keep our momentum and it will carry us part-way up the hill without any effort. You can do that." Then, picking out another uphill marker, I said, "Let's make it up to that bend in the road. I don't care how slow we go, just make it." Breathing heavily, Chris pressed on. When we reached the bend in the road, I said, "It's just a little bit farther to the top of the hill." "Okay, you worked this hard, let's let gravity take us down to the bottom of the hill." Down we went.

At the bottom of the hill, Chris gasped, "That's it! No more! I cannot go any farther. I am dropping out." "Okay Chris,

96

if that is what you want, but see that clearing just ahead, that is the clearing at the end of the trail." Chris looked up; and his eyes widened. He turned to Ed Anderson and said, "Ed, we made it! There is the clearing! We made it!"

It was a good lesson about putting out a bit of extra effort, even when you are physically exhausted. It can make a big difference.

They made it, indeed. Chris went on to serve with the Pioneer Battalion at Camp Pendleton and Ed served in Vietnam as a helicopter pilot.

THE D.I

In the 1950s, *Dragnet* was one of the most popular programs on television. Every show began the same way. There was a panorama of a smoggy city skyline, and then a deadpan voice intoned, "This is the city... I work here... I am a cop. My name is Friday." Actor Jack Webb played the part of police sergeant Joe Friday, a slender, unflappable man, who insisted that his job was to get the facts, "just the facts." It is unlikely that there was a policeman in the United States more popular than Joe Friday. Then, in 1957, Joe Friday joined the Marines. Jack Webb directed and starred in a movie called, *"The D.I."*

The letters "D.I." are an abbreviation for "drill instructor," the noncommissioned officer who is charged with the duty of ramrodding raw recruits through a tough three-month boot camp designed to shape those recruits into Marines. Jack Webb played the part of Gunnery Sergeant Jim Moore, who brought the unflappable persona of Joe Friday to a Marine Corps drill instructor. Gunny Moore was reputed to be the toughest D.I. in the Marine Recruit Depot at Parris Island, S.C. In the movie, Moore is exposed to pressure from above and below. Private Owens, a recruit in Moore's platoon, performs at an unacceptably low level despite having what appears to be outstanding intelligence and superior physical ability. Moore takes Owens' intransigence as a personal challenge. In the meanwhile, Moore's

99

commanding officer is worried that Owens' erratic performance will reflect poorly on the platoon as a whole. He virtually orders Moore to dismiss Owens from the Corps. Sgt. Moore refuses to give up on Owens.

Instead, Moore increases the pressure on Owens, particularly when Owens seriously considers running away from the recruit depot. In one scene filmed near the recruit barracks, Sgt. Moore points to the tidal swamp surrounding the island, and tells Owens that no one has ever made it out alive. In the end, the D.I. prevails. Owens changes his outlook, and becomes a part of a successful platoon. If only real life was as easy as the movie.

In April 1956, the year before the movie, another Parris Island D.I. attempted to discipline his recruit platoon by leading them in a night march through Ribbon Creek, behind the rifle range. Staff Sergeant Matthew McKeon led the way. He figured that if the platoon followed closely in his footsteps, no one would encounter deep water. It did not go as planned. Ribbon Creek is a tidal swamp in which the water level changes abruptly from shallow to deep without any visible warning. The platoon did not keep a tight line of march. The rear elements strayed out of line; and six Marines drowned.

The tragedy was compounded by Marine Corps Commandant, General Randolph McCall Pate, who declared the D.I. guilty of manslaughter, and then ordered that McKeon be confined to the brig and court-martialed. The public news media went wild. Newspapers, radio and television called for McKeon's head. Then, Jack Webb's movie, "The D.I.," was released and public opinion began to swing in favor of Sgt. McKeon. The court martial remained front page news; but a majority of the public cheered when the court martial board rejected the charge of involuntary manslaughter and found Sgt. McKeon guilty of only the lesser charge of negligent homicide.

In September 1959, when we reported for the 25th Officer Candidates Course at Marine Corps Base, Quantico, Virginia, the "Ribbon Creek Incident" was fresh in our minds. Also, many of us had read Leon Uris' description of boot camp in his best-selling novel, *"Battle Cry."* We knew that the Marine Corps' basic training methods had changed, but we did not know the extent of those changes, and how that would affect the officer candidates program. Most of us heard horror stories from our friends who went through boot camp at Parris Island while we were in college. Now we were assembled in one of those tin butler huts behind our barracks. It was set up like a theater. I couldn't believe my eyes. The Marine striding up to the microphone looked just like Jack Webb. But it was not Jack Webb; and he was not our D.I. He was the company commander, Captain Mike White. Still, the resemblance to Jack Webb was unsettling.

We had already met our D.I.s – there were two of them. They played the roles of "nice D.I. – tough D.I." The nice D.I. was Gunnery Sgt. Robert L. DeBruhl, whose official title was "platoon sergeant." DeBruhl was tall, tanned, and had a photogenic appearance that is usually seen only in recruiting posters. The tough guy was Sgt. Franklin R. Alender, our "sergeant instructor." Alender was on the short side, stocky and well muscled. He delighted in regaling the platoon with stories of his exploits as a high school athlete in Kentucky. If one thing was clear to the 45 members of the second platoon of Charlie Company, it was that Sgt. Alender was dead set on driving anyone he chose out of the officer candidates program and into the pits of Parris Island and the tidal swamps of Ribbon Creek. Alender was our enemy-in-chief.

Like *Alice in Wonderland*, it began at the beginning. In the wee hours of our first morning in Quantico, Sgt. Alender awakened the entire platoon with a deafening racket caused by running a glass Coke bottle around the inside of a galvanized metal GI can. It continued months later when he ran through our overnight bivouac at Kopp's farm, yelling "Atomic attack! Move out!" Bill Harrison was so intimidated that night, he snapped to the position of full attention, forgetting that he was in a low-slung pup tent at the time.

Some barbs were personal. "Blum, how old are you?" "How did you get so f----n' ugly in just twenty-five years?" Ron Roe made the mistake of walking out of the shower and directly into the squadbay with his towel across his shoulder. Alender ordered Ron to stand on his foot locker while the entire platoon trooped by and patted him on his bare butt.

The closest we came to a physical altercation was that afternoon when we were scrubbing down the squadbay deck. To make the work more bearable, we sang as we scrubbed: college songs, drinking songs, spirituals, military songs – anything. Sgt. Alender was in the platoon office, squaring away his dress uniform. We were starting to sing military songs. One of the first songs was "The Caissons Go Rolling Along." Hardly had we begun when Sgt. Alender, dressed in khaki trousers and a white T-shirt, burst into the room, screaming, "Stop it! That's a "doggie" song! We don't sing no "doggie" songs." I tried, but I could not hold it back. I burst into laughter – and Alender saw me.

Shouting epithets and challenges, he charged across the room, stopping inches from my face. I was sure that this was the end of my officer candidate experience. At this point, my only goal was to avoid being the one who threw the first punch. Alender reached out quickly with his right hand. Was it a punch? No, he grabbed the chain of the miraculous medal that I wore around my neck. I moved my open hands forward, so as to be in a position to respond to any assault that might come. I did not know how this was going to play out, but I was not going to be a punching bag. We stared at each other for about twenty seconds, and then he let go of the chain. The confrontation was over. That was a long time ago.

In recent years, the surviving members of our officer candidate platoon have been able to reestablish contact with each other thanks to the computer.  In 2009, we planned a reunion of the platoon at the Officers Candidate School, in Quantico on the 50th anniversary of the time that we reported for duty in the Marine Corps. Our biggest surprise in the planning was an e-mail message from Ron Roe in California. Ron had located Sgt. Alender, who was now a retired gunnery sergeant, living in Cary, North Carolina. Everyone agreed that we should invite "Frank" Alender to attend the reunion as the guest of the platoon.

The reunion began with a note of uncertainty. Alender had not seen or heard from any of us for more than fifty years. Similarly, we had no idea what he now looked like. When we entered the Crossroads Inn, we all saw the old guy by the lobby door, wearing a white T-shirt and a freshly starched and ironed utility cap. Is that him? Indeed it was.

Once we opened the conference room that we reserved, things got easier. As more and more people talked to Frank, he began to recall our 1959 platoon. The first day of the program, he and DeBruhl went through our files and came to the conclusion that we had a good chance to become the Honor Platoon. One member of the platoon remembered that Frank did not attend our commissioning ceremony. Frank's infant son died at about that time, and Frank was fully absorbed in that tragic event. The platoon member saluted Frank, and handed him a silver dollar – a tradition usually observed at the commissioning ceremonies.

At the current Officers Candidate School, we were given a presentation by the commanding officer. The officers and staff were surprised to learn that these 25 visitors were members of a single platoon that went through the program fifty years ago. Even more surprising to them was the fact that we brought with us one of our D.I.s. When we posed for a photo in front of the present day OCS, Frank held the pennant indicating that we were from Charlie Company. Back at the Crossroads, other Marines made it a point to approach Frank and tell him that he did a great job with "that group back there." Frank had one helluva good time.

After the reunion, Frank wrote a "thank-you" letter, and made several follow-up phone calls. He asked for background material on the members of the platoon, and was appreciative when he received it. Two men sent him copies of Tim Geraghty's book on the Marine Barracks in Beirut. He donated one of the copies to his local library. Frank received frequent notes and phone calls from members of our group. In late 2011, I received a phone call from Leo Carlin. He said that phone calls to Frank were not answered; and that he did a Google search and found an obituary. Our D.I. died on November 5, 2011. Frank probably was angry that he did not make it another five days until the Marine Corps birthday.

Not long ago, General Colin Powell was quoted to the effect that, "No one ever forgets the name of his drill instructor." Frank Alender would take issue with that contention. After all, what does Colin Powell know about drill instructors? Powell was a "doggie."

THE CANNON AT PICKEL MEADOW

The assignment to attend a cold weather training course at Pickel Meadow was not well received. It was January 1961. Ten years earlier, prompted by the bitter cold and inhospitable mountain terrain of the Chosin Reservoir in North Korea, the U.S. Marine Corps sought a place to prepare Marines to deal with those elements. The place they chose became the Mountain Warfare Training Center, near Bridgeport, California, in the High Sierras. Most Marines refer to it by reference to a prominent terrain feature, Pickel Meadow. It is a place of 12,000-foot heights, 20+ foot snows, and subzero temperatures in the winter. The National Forest Service told the Marines that the land was uninhabitable for most of the year. It was exactly what the Marines were looking for. The training center opened in 1951. By 1961, it was a legend throughout the Fleet Marine Force. My assignment provoked a lot of teasing from my cohorts in San Clemente, California. I went along with the crowd; every chance that I got, I griped about the impending Icelandic experience.

When the fateful day arrived, I awoke early; and quietly left the apartment without waking my roommate Ed Clifford or Richie Straehle who was staying with us until he found his own place. It was still dark when I arrived at the Camp Pendleton air strip. There, I joined twenty or more Marines for what turned out to be about a two-hour flight to an air facility in Nevada. There, we boarded trucks and drove west into the mountains. After an hour or so, we went by a large lake. Someone said that it was Lake Tahoe. What a pretty place! Had we taken a vote, the truck would have stopped right there. But we had orders, and the orders told us to continue on Route 395 for about an hour to Bridgeport, and then a few miles west to Pickel Meadow.

The headquarters was a wood frame building that looked like it had seen better days. Quickly, we were assigned to separate groups of about a dozen Marines each, and directed to canvas tents that would be our quarters for the next week (or at least that part of the week when we were in camp). About ten of us shared a tent with a potbelly stove in the middle. We were told that we had to keep a close eye on the stovepipe. After a while, the pipe would glow red – and the next thing you know, the canvas of the tent would be in flames. We paid attention to what we were told. On occasion, the fringes of our tent started to smolder, but we quickly cut back on the stove's fuel. Despite the best efforts of the potbelly stove, the tent was very cold – and getting colder. The obvious alternative was to spread your sleeping bag on a cot, and then crawl into the bag for the night. It took only a few minutes for your body heat to warm the sleeping bag. Then, the question was, how much of your clothing you would bring into the bag with you for the night. For most of us, the answer to that question did not come until the morning.

Almost all of us had our utility trousers and jacket in the sleeping bag all night. Socks were a different story. You wanted them to air out over the night. On the other hand, if you left the socks overnight on the deck, in the morning it was like pulling two large ice cubes over your feet. Many of us resolved this question by leaving the socks out at night, but we pulled them inside the sleeping bag when we awoke, and let them warm up for a few minutes. A bigger question was what to do with the boots? In the bag? Or out of the bag? As best I can recall, I tried both alternatives. On the mornings that my boots were outside the bag, I set my personal best record for the high-jump from the seated position.

As might be expected of a remote and difficult base, the mess hall was outstanding. Nutrition was a high priority. My clearest memory of the Pickel Meadow mess hall is its stock of buttermilk in the refrigerators at the entrance. I had not seen buttermilk since I was in sixth grade. When they give you buttermilk, you know that they want you to survive.

When it came to survival tactics, we were taught to use cross-country skis and snowshoes. We learned about the expected onslaught of cold weather storms, and how to avoid the major dangers of those elements. We built snow caves and lean-tos. Much to my surprise, the radiant heat of the sun was more than enough to keep us warm in the low humidity of the High Sierras. I was also surprised when we were warned not to drink the fast running water of Wolf Creek. Recent tests of the water showed the presence of liver flukes. The warning had little effect. An overwhelming majority of Marines preferred the Wolf Creek "flukes" over the tap water at the base camp. The cold weather course turned out to be a great vacation. However, after all of the griping I had done back in San Clemente, I was not about to tell my friends what I great time I had at Pickel Meadow. As things turned out, very few people wanted to hear my experience after Larry Heilman told them about the lost cannon.

Larry looked like a teenage poster-boy for Southern California; not at all like a man with a graduate degree in archaeology on a career path to a doctorate. He used to say that he joined the Marine Corps so that when he returned to graduate school he would look more like what people expected of a doctoral candidate. Larry attended the summer version of the

mountain warfare course. In the summer, they focused on the hazardous mountain terrain. Larry was at Pickel Meadow for only a day or two when a few of his friends decided to play a practical joke. They positioned themselves close to Larry's bunk where he was sure to overhear their conversation.

"Did you hear about Chuck this afternoon? He was conducting squad maneuvers near Lost Cannon Peak, when one of the Marines slipped and fell down into a ravine. When a rescue party went down to get him, they saw what looked like a large piece of metal protruding from the rocks. They couldn't see the whole thing because it was buried tight. Chuck said that it looked like the barrel of a civil war cannon. We are going back up there Saturday to dig it out."

Cautiously, they looked over at Larry's bunk but Larry was no longer there. He had taken the bait and run with it.

Larry knew the story of Colonel John C. Fremont, who led a small expedition across the High Sierras in 1844. Fremont was a tough guy. All of his men were fighters. They had with them a small mountain howitzer. It was mounted on a two-wheel carriage pulled by a mule. It looked like the baby brother of one of those civil war cannons that you see at many military parks. The barrel was just a bit over three feet long; and it weighed about 225 pounds. Caught in a heavy snowstorm in the rugged mountains, Fremont was forced to abandon his cannon in order to get out with their lives. Now, Larry had visions of being the man who found Fremont's lost cannon after more than 115 years.

It was about an hour later when Larry's friends caught up with him in the mess hall. Larry's bright red face was bursting with excitement. The words fairly tumbled out of his mouth as he told them about overhearing their conversation and realizing the importance of this historic discovery. His friends smiled as Larry rambled on — until Larry said, "I just got off the phone with the chairman of archaeology studies at the University of California. They are organizing a team of experts and will be here sometime tomorrow to dig the cannon out of the hills." The immediate change in the facial expressions of his audience told Larry that something was amiss. They knew that they had to "fess up," and fess up quick, so that there would be time to call off the university expedition. For Larry it was an embarrassing ordeal; but for me years later, it is hard not to laugh.

This story came to mind in the spring of 2011, as I was planning a vacation trip to Lake Tahoe and Yosemite which would take us right past Pickel Meadow. Apparently, people are still looking for Fremont's cannon. One website says that some of the metal parts of the carriage were found near Lost Cannon Peak in 2005. That website also disputes a claim by a museum in Carson City that it has the barrel of the cannon on display. It says that the barrel of Fremont's cannon is still out there near Pickel Meadow, waiting to be found.

I never did get a close look at those cannon parts. When we reached the Bridgeport ranger station, it was Memorial Day. The station was closed. The metal parts of the cannon carriage were in a display case that was barely visible from the window of the front door. We could not stay any longer. That distant glimpse of Fremont's cannon was the best that I could do. About a week later, we came across Fremont's glass punchbowl in a museum in Mariposa. No, it was not filled with fish house punch – not even buttermilk.

A WHITE TOP WARRIOR

The morning was cold, and dark, and dreary. The rain was a light drizzle, almost a spray, but it was persistent. As I turned into the southbound lanes of Interstate-95 preparing myself for the 140-mile drive to Arlington National Cemetery, the rain and the intermittent flicking of the windshield wipers brought to mind an old memory from the time when I first met Bill Waters.

It was September 1959, and we were part of the Marine Corps' 25th Officer Candidates Course, in Quantico, Virginia. Forty-five of us were designated as the second platoon of Charlie Company. We had no prior contact with each other. We came from all parts of the country; and none of us knew what to expect in the days to come. Some men from the western states were not used to the high humidity that enveloped them in Quantico. Nostalgically, they said that back home in California and Texas the weather is pretty hot, but it is a "dry heat," and you really don't mind it. Bill Waters chimed in, "I am from Colorado, and back there it gets pretty cold up in the mountains, but it's a dry cold, and you really don't mind it." I could not resist the temptation. I said, "Back in Philadelphia, we get a lot of rain but it is a dry rain, and you really don't mind it." Bill Waters anticipated the punch line, and broke into laughter before I spoke the words. That sense of humor carried us through the officers program and beyond.

For a randomly-selected group, we got along very well. In fact, at the end of the program we were designated the "honor platoon." After being commissioned Second Lieutenants, we went our separate ways. More than forty years later, with the advent of the Internet, we re-connected with each other at occasional reunions in Quantico. For our 50th anniversary, Bill Waters volunteered to coordinate a visit to HMX-1, a helicopter squadron based at Quantico. Part of the mission of HMX-1 is to provide helicopter transportation to the President of the United States. These are special helicopters, painted Marine Corps green in the body, and the top part painted white. They are known as "White Tops." At one point in his career, Bill had been assigned to HMX-1, where he transported Presidents Lyndon Johnson and Richard Nixon – albeit not at the same time. Bill was hoping that he could get us a tour of the White Tops. It did not work out. We were given an outstanding display and demonstration of the other helicopters, but when it came to the White Tops we settled for a video presentation. Bill was disappointed, but he understood the security concerns involved.

Meanwhile, I continued south on I-95 despite the rain and the darkness. I left Philadelphia extra early because I remembered the difficulty we had two years ago at Jim Tully's burial. Bill Waters drove that time. He told Charley Smith and me that he knew his way around Arlington. He knew where all of the gates were located, and how to get to them. He knew that indeed. The problem was that all of those gates were locked. We barely made it to Jim's burial. While we were there, Bill told us of his plans to be buried in Arlington. I told him that I would come down for the ceremony if I was still alive and able to travel. Now, I was still alive and I knew how to get to Arlington's main gate; but Bill's burial was not scheduled to start at the main gate. It would start at the Ft. Myers Memorial Chapel. A Google search of Ft. Myers gave me a route to the chapel – but it was the only route I had. I had two hours to spare when I stopped at a rest area near the Washington beltway. Unfortunately, the beltway was jammed with traffic. Nearly two hours ticked away by the time that I reached Ft. Myers. By that time the rain had stopped.

 Outlined against the gray rain clouds and morning sky were two platoons of Marines and a squad from the band, standing in formation in front of the chapel door. They were wearing raincoats. Inside the chapel, a dozen or so family members sat in the pews on the right front. On the left were scattered groups of two or three people, some of them wearing Marine Corps dress blues. The chaplain was speaking, and nearing the end of his remarks. When he concluded, the organ struck up two choruses of "Eternal Father," and then the flag-draped casket was rolled down the center aisle

and we were on our way out to join the honor guard. The band and the two platoons of Marines led the way, followed by the horse-drawn caisson, followed by six or seven cars. Mine was the third car in the line.

The cortege moved slowly through the gate and wound east down Porter Drive near the Tomb of the Unknown Soldier, and then further downhill where the road becomes Bradley Drive. A Marine guard was stationed at each crossing to stop cross-traffic. The cortege stopped on Bradley Drive about forty yards before the Columbarium, a large group of concrete structures

designed to hold thousands of funeral urns. Pallbearers from the honor guard lifted the casket on their shoulders and marched left, to the center of a large open field. For a moment, I felt sorry for the members of the honor guard who had to march through that soggy grass and mud wearing their spit-shined dress shoes. This certainly had not been a dry rain. My sympathy evaporated when

I realized that I would have to follow in their footsteps. As we walked across that grassy quagmire, I was struck by the irony that Bill's nickname is "Muddy."

The band and the honor guard took up formation in the open area between the casket and the Columbarium. Seven riflemen positioned themselves about 100 yards beyond the casket. There were seats for Beth Waters and some of the immediate family. The rest of us gathered close by for the final blessing. The riflemen snapped off a 21-gun salute (three volleys of seven rifles each). As usual, it sounded as though there were three single shots. One of the buglers from the band played Taps.

There was a flag-folding ceremony and the folded flag was presented to Beth Waters by the Lieutenant Colonel in charge of the burial unit. Also, a Colonel and a Sergeant-major offered their condolences to the Waters family. At that point, the honor guard made a left-face, and marched back to Bradley Drive.

Family and friends remained gathered around the casket, consoling one another. Two friends placed their wing medals on the casket. At about this time, we heard the unmistakable staccato sound of helicopters in the distance. The sound grew louder, and everyone looked up. Flying from the direction of the White House, and skirting the southeast corner of the cemetery were three White Top helicopters. The White Top fly-over was the final salute.

Semper Fi, Bill!

ANSLEY HORTON

We last saw each other 49 years ago at the Marine Corps Base in Quantico, Virginia. We were part of the 2nd Platoon, Charlie Company, the Honor Platoon of the 25th Officer Candidates Course. Remember how Sgt. Alender reacted to your first name? "Gawd!! Your parents played one hellluva joke on you, didn't they?"

You were ranked sixth out of the 321 candidates in that program. That was pretty good. In December 1959, we went our separate ways. You went helicoptering; and I took an advanced course in ground pounding.

Thanks to the personal computer, we resumed contact over the past few years. Unfortunately, medical complications kept you from joining us in Quantico for our recent reunions. We'll miss you at our 50th next September.

We'll tell everyone that you are part of the advance party handling the logistics for our final get-together. By the way, I notice that you did not name any of your children "Ansley."

THE PADRE

Talk about self-conscious! It was August 1960; I was a second lieutenant fresh out of Officers' Basic School; and I was reporting to my first duty station in the United States Marine Corps. I looked like hell.

Two weeks earlier, there was an automobile accident in the Arizona desert that required surgery to repair a broken cheekbone. Upon my release from Balboa Naval Hospital, I was reunited with my uniforms that had been in the back of the car and then crated up and shipped to San Diego, California. The uniform jacket did not look too bad but my shirts and ties looked as though they had been through a food processor. Fortunately, my jacket covered most of my crumpled shirt, and all except the knot of my tie. At Camp Pendleton, the Adjutant asked whether I would be more comfortable on that hot day if I took off my jacket. "No thank you sir, I am comfortable with the jacket on," I lied. I suspect that the Adjutant doubted my sanity but I was afraid that if he saw my full dress shirt and tie, I would be sent to the brig. The Adjutant processed my orders and directed me to report to the First Antitank Battalion at Camp Horno, about twenty miles away in the northern part of Pendleton.

About an hour later, I walked into the Antitank Battalion headquarters at Camp Horno and was told that the commanding officer, Colonel Sexton, would see me but I would have to wait. Colonel Sexton was then meeting with the battalion chaplain, whose name I cannot recall. "Please have a seat," said the battalion clerk.

Much to my surprise, I was summoned almost immediately into the colonel's office. Colonel Sexton introduced me to the chaplain. He then explained to the chaplain that he had important matters to discuss with me and he ushered the chaplain to the door. The chaplain departed and I was alone with Colonel Sexton. I wondered what "important matters" the Colonel had in mind. I was not important; I was a brand new second lieutenant. Until an hour ago, neither of us knew that I would be assigned to the battalion. As the door closed behind the chaplain, Sexton said, "Thank God, you came when you did! I thought that I would never get rid of him." I was stunned. I thought that chaplains were universally admired. Over the next few years, I learned different. There are chaplains and there are Chaplains. Some chaplains were in the service for their own self-interest, and others were there to serve the spiritual needs of the Marines. The officers of the battalion did not appreciate the first mentioned type of chaplain. On the other hand, the chaplains that were there to serve the Marines were highly appreciated by all.

Recently, Bob Powers called my attention to the story of Chaplain Vincent R. Capodanno. Chaplain Capodanno is the subject of a book titled "The Grunt Padre." He served with the

5th Marines and the 7th Marines in Vietnam. He was posthumously awarded the Medal of Honor and is presently a candidate for canonization. After reading the book, I mentioned Capodanno's name to Father Bob (Bagel) Breen, an archdiocesan priest who spent a lot of time as chaplain to various college sports teams, including the Philadelphia Big Five basketball program. I was surprised when Bagel said, "I have heard of him. He was a loose cannon." Bagel had been told, presumably by one of the priests at the retirement villa, that Capodanno flouted authority and that the Marine Corps "could not keep him out of the aircraft during combat missions." That did not sound right. Maybe some of the other chaplains were afraid that they too would be expected to accompany Marines in combat.

I sent an e-mail message to the members of my 1959 Officer Candidate platoon, asking if anyone knew Chaplain Capodanno. There were four responses, each one glowing with praise. Three of the respondents specifically mentioned meeting Chaplain Capodanno under combat conditions. Tim Geraghty stated that it was the regimental commander who nominated Capodanno for the Medal of Honor, and personally followed up on that recommendation. *The Grunt Padre* notes that another one of Capodanno's strong supporters was John Cardinal O'Connor, himself a former Navy chaplain in Vietnam. That does not sound like a "loose cannon." When I mentioned that support to Bagel, he backed off his comment. I gave him my copy of the book.

MEANING NO DISRESPECT

It is an introductory clause that is second nature to most Marines. They must teach it at the Recruit Depot in Parris Island. Disrespect of an officer is bad, very bad. Even the rawest recruit knows that he should not diss an officer. And so, when the inevitable difference of opinion arises, the reasonably prudent Marine prefaces his remarks as follows, "Meaning no disrespect, sir." And how does the Marine officer react to that diplomatic form of address which he hears day after day from any one of the hundred or so Marines in his command? What the officer hears is, "Look here you horse's ass!"

SEA WORLD REDUX

The conventional wisdom is that "you cannot go back." Yet, recently I found myself driving south to San Diego's

SeaWorld, just as I did in November 1960, fifty years ago. There were five of us back then, Ed Clifford, Jack Carew, Jay Baxter, Bob Lohr and me. We were lieutenants in the United States Marine Corps, stationed at Camp Pendleton, California. We lived in apartments in nearby San Clemente. It was Thanksgiving Day, and we were a long way from home. My family was in Philadelphia. The others were from New York. There was no way that any of us could get home for the holiday, so we decided to celebrate by driving to SeaWorld, and then returning to San Clemente to cook our own Thanksgiving dinner.

In May 2013, the highway approach to SeaWorld was still recognizable. The winding roadway weaves in and out through a series of ponds or small lakes. Road signs clearly mark the route to the entrance of SeaWorld; yet, something had changed. I don't recall having been charged $15 in 1960 for the privilege of parking our car in a distant parking lot. Similarly, the admission charge of

$78 per person was totally out of sync with the economics of 1960 (and we did not qualify for a senior discount back then). Moreover, in 1960 there were no credit cards, ATM machines or computerized ticketing devices. We paid cash on the barrelhead to a live ticket seller. In 2013, they had our money in no time at all.

There were also major substantive differences. In 1960, SeaWorld was a first-class aquarium. In effect, it was an aquatic zoo. There were specimens of a wide variety of sea life, some of which were trained to perform acrobatics. The most impressive display was the group of dolphins that simultaneously leaped more than ten feet out of the water at an unseen command. We were impressed.

The present-day SeaWorld is a theme park, much like Disneyworld, Busch Gardens and Hershey Park. Instead of just one aquatic theater at which all specimens are presented, SeaWorld now has five separate theaters (they call them "stadiums"), each dedicated to particular types of sea life, i.e., killer whales, dolphins, sea lions etcetera. The star attractions today are the killer whales. It is astonishing to see something the size of a school bus leap out of the water and high into the air. A new theater of human acrobats from the Cirque du Soleil is being introduced as the Cirque de la Mer. Also, carnival-type rides and restaurants are scattered throughout the grounds. One of the current food items that would have been greatly appreciated on that Thanksgiving Day in 1960, is a smoked turkey leg (priced at about $9 per). It looked great.

Back in 1960, we had nothing like that for Thanksgiving dinner. Our menu looked traditional. It included roast turkey, stuffing, cranberry sauce, and mashed potatoes, preceded by an abundance of frozen daiquiris. However, with the exception of the daiquiris, all of the food was C-rations. We had three very large olive-drab cans, and two smaller ones. The contents were stenciled in black paint on the sides. The cans looked like they had been stored for years in some remote corner of a concrete warehouse. I forget who came up with the C-rations, but it was not me. I suspect that it was either Baxter or Carew.

 Ed Clifford and I volunteered the use of our patio, on top of the cliffs overlooking the Pacific. Ed also had a hand in making the mashed potatoes. I handled the daiquiris, which proved very popular. My main concern with the daiquiris was that one of our number might lose his balance and go reeling over the cliff. Fortunately, that did not happen.

The highlight of the meal was the C-rations. Sometimes your present experience presages something that is to occur later in time. So it was with the C-ration turkey. Two years later, we were part of an amphibious landing on the island of Mindoro in the Philippines. The native people who lived in that rugged bush country were called "Negritos." The Negritos tried to teach us how to live off the land in such an unforgiving place. One of their tips was about finding edible food in places where there seemed to be no life. The trick was in finding a growth of large bamboo plants. In the daytime, these shoots could be cut down, and often a nocturnal bat would be found crammed inside the open top of the cylindrical plant. In the absence of dark caves, bats often used bamboo shoots as a place to sleep during the day. The bat looked for all the world like a very thin turkey in a bamboo can that was one size too small. It was hardly the stuff of a Thanksgiving dinner. Back in San Clemente, I kept our Thanksgiving turkey at arms' length, and made myself another daiquiri. It was a meal that none of us ever forgot.

With that repast in mind, I left SeaWorld behind in 2013, and headed straight for Berta's restaurant in Old City San Diego. We should have done that fifty years ago.

MAYFAIR PRESBYTERIANS

It is hard to remember what the Mayfair Presbyterian Church looked like when I first moved to Mayfair, but the dignified stone church was not part of it. Mayfair Presbyterian was a work in progress. The pastor's house was three blocks away. It was right across the driveway behind my house. The corner house on my block of Chippendale Avenue was owned by Joe Casacio. He built the Mayfair Presbyterian Church. Joe must have been a pretty good builder. The stone church was a first-class building. It looked like a church ought to look. Joe Casacio continued building houses, converting them into apartment units, and then starting all over again. "I didn't know it was so easy to make money," he said.

I did not have much personal contact with the Presbyterian Church even though I lived in the neighborhood for nearly thirty years. In the early 1940s, Catholics were treated as a religious and social minority. We stuck together. We had our own schools and our own athletic leagues, as well as our own churches. We were discouraged from participating in the services of other churches for fear that we would give the impression we were not satisfied with our own church. Mr. Henderson was the pastor of Mayfair Presbyterian Church. He did not wear black clerical clothing; nor did he wear the celluloid Roman collars that we always associated with priests. He was reserved and soft-spoken.

Years later, when television came on the scene, there was a character called "Mr. Rogers" who reminded me of Mr. Henderson, except that Mr. Henderson did not wear cardigan sweaters. Mr. Henderson was surprised when my mother told him that my brother Jack and I would attend his church's summer Bible School. When reminded of the Archdiocese's stance against participating in the programs of other churches, Mom said, "I don't agree with that. They pretty much believe in the same things that we do. Besides, it won't hurt you." She was right.

For the next two months, Jack and I attended the Mayfair Presbyterian Church Bible School on two days of each week. It was interesting. We used a children's-level "Bible Stories" book. It had a lot of drawings. The teacher would read stories about people like Samson, Noah, Moses and Solomon, after which we would talk about them. Mr. Henderson was not involved in most of the school activities, but he was present for the start and the end of each school day. Generally, he would make a few light comments and then say a prayer with his arms outstretched and head bowed. It was interesting to see Mr. Henderson in the church environment. They called him "Reverend." He was still the same quiet man that he was in the neighborhood, but he was clearly the person in charge of the church. Years later, I would think about that summer school as being the start of my appreciation for the Bible. On the other hand, it did little for my appreciation of Joe Casacio's building skills. I paid no attention to the construction features or the room layout of the church.

About a dozen years after the Bible school, I had another opportunity to be inside the Mayfair Presbyterian Church. Ray Block was one of the few persons I knew who was a member of that church. Ray is about five years older than me. He was an organizer. He organized a variety of youth baseball, basketball and football teams, mainly under the name "Mayfair A.C." Ray did not play for any of those teams; he was strictly an organizer, manager, and coach. However, on occasion Ray would put together a basketball team comprised of his friends. I was not one of his friends.

It was not clear whether this basketball team was sponsored by the church. Most of their games were played in the basement of Mayfair Presbyterian Church. On the other hand, most of the players, including Fred Eisele and my brother Jack, were not Presbyterians. One afternoon, Ray could scrape up only four players; he needed a fifth. After exhausting all other possibilities, he told Fred Eisele that it would be okay to ask me to be the fifth man. I don't know why Ray did not ask me directly. Maybe it was because I was not one of his friends.

The basement gym was pretty much what you might expect of a basement gym – but still, I was impressed. It was Joe Casacio's gym; a bit on the dark side, but it had plenty of overhead space. I did not recognize any of the players on the opposing team. I took that as a good sign because it meant they did not know me either. They would have to assume that I knew my way around a basketball court unless I proved otherwise.

Hardly had the game started when I knew something was wrong. I could see it; I could feel it. The gym was getting darker. I had the ball and was dribbling to my right, past Ray Block. Suddenly, Ray disappeared from view. My range of vision was constricting. It was like being in a tunnel except that the edges were not sharply defined. What looked like a small strand of barbed wire glowed white near the lower edge of the tunnel. My peripheral vision was gone. I was frightened but I dared not say anything. Maybe it would go away. It was my first experience with what people call "ocular migraines." Those events involve electrical storms in the brain and restriction of blood flow to the optic nerve. Typically, there is a temporary loss of vision in one or both eyes.

I suffered in silence, hoping my vision would improve; but the gym was getting darker. I decided to get rid of the ball as quickly as possible whenever it came to me. Fred took a short step in my direction. I looked right at him and passed the ball sharply while I could still see him. Fred was having a good game shooting jump shots from the corner of the court. Meanwhile, George Herrmann drove the ball up the foul lane like he owned it. I was not surprised when the player who was guarding me dropped back to double team Fred and George. It occurred to me that he would continue that tactic unless he thought that I was a scoring threat. I had to shoot the ball. The opportunity came soon enough. We were breaking toward our own basket. George was on the left; Fred was on the right. All the defenders dropped back, leaving me wide open for a short jump shot. I was looking straight at the basket. I did not dare to turn my head. It was a shot that I could make in my sleep – and that was pretty much the case. The ball was in the net before the opposing team knew what happened. No one was happier than I when we reached the half-time break.

The break gave me a chance to rest my eyes for about fifteen minutes. That short rest was just what the doctor ordered. My vision improved gradually during the second half. In the meanwhile, Fred and George carried our team offensively. I never mentioned the ocular migraine to anyone. After the game, Ray Block told Fred that I had "played a good game." I couldn't say; I didn't see much of it. Good game or not, I was never invited to play in another one of Ray's games. That one game ended my experience with Mayfair's Presbyterians.

A few years ago, I published a book that set out in short-story fashion many of my memories. One of those memories was about Ray Block and his organization of youth athletic teams under the names "Mayfair A.C." and "Mayfair Monarchs." At Fred Eisele's suggestion, I sent a copy of the book to Ray. A few weeks later, I received a handwritten note from Ray thanking me for sending him "that nice little book."

Last year I came across a death notice for Ray Block. His funeral was to be held at Mayfair Presbyterian Church. Ray was 82 years of age, unmarried, and had no surviving family. The members of our basement basketball team of years ago now live in places far removed from the Philadelphia area. Still, the church was crowded with about 180 mourners, mostly former players and parents of players on the youth athletic teams Ray had organized over the years. It was an impressive turnout.

At the end of the ceremony, the funeral director rolled the casket out of the church and down a ramp to the waiting hearse. It was only then the undertaker realized that no pallbearers had been selected. He looked at his two assistants, and he looked at the space over which the casket had to be lifted, and then he called out to me as I was walking to my car, "Excuse me, could you give us a hand with the casket?" Of course I could – and did. And that is how I came to be a pallbearer for my old friend Ray Block.

MESSAGES

Messages are important. The Oxford Universal dictionary defines messages as "an oral or written communication from one person to another." In the days of cowboys and Indians movies, American Indians communicated by way of smoke signals, informing their cohorts of the approach of wagon trains or units of mounted cavalry. The cavalry was more advanced; they communicated by telegraph and Morse code. Hardly a movie passed without an Indian climbing a pole in the middle of the alkalai desert to cut a telegraph wire. In the Second World War, Navajo Indian "code talkers" transmitted combat messages in their own native language which was incomprehensible to the opposing Japanese forces.

In our neighborhood, we picked up the importance of sending messages. Jack Donaghy and Lou Griffin lived directly across the driveway from each other. They stretched a string across the driveway, from Lou's bedroom to Jack's. Each end the string was attached to an empty soup can. They would shout into the can, and the message was carried by vibrations along the string from one can to the other. The message was also plainly audible to everyone else on the block, but that did not seem to matter at the time. It was like the "Message to Garcia;" it got through.

LETTERS TO HARRY

Harry Silcox has been a part of northeast Philadelphia for as long as I can remember. He grew up in Tacony. When Lincoln High School opened in 1950, Harry played on its basketball team. He did not look like much. He was tall and skinny and his hair

looked as though he had just touched a live electrical outlet. He reminded me of Reddi Kilowatt, the Philadelphia Electric Company's cartoon personification. However, Harry's team usually won the game. Silcox went on to play basketball for the legendary coach Harry Litwack at Temple University. After college, Harry returned to Lincoln High, first as a basketball coach, and later became principal of the school. During his career path, he developed an intense interest in the history of the northeast Philadelphia neighborhoods in which he was born and raised. In the process, he became the preeminent historian of those neighborhoods.

Although Harry and I grew up in adjacent neighborhoods, we met for the first time in 2008 at a lunch gathering of the Old Timers Bats & Balls group. Since that time, I have joined Harry as a member of the Trustees of Lower Dublin Academy (which carries out a part of the will of Thomas Holme, William Penn's surveyor) and as a participant in the meetings of several history groups in the northeast. Our historical interests are similar, but our backgrounds and writing styles are different. Harry has done a wealth of first-hand research on the neighborhoods; whereas I have focused on Philadelphia's legal community. Moreover, Harry has his memories, and I have mine. Our differing perspectives naturally led to differing views on some of the subjects of Harry's books and articles.

In 2009, I received an e-mail message from Harry telling me about an article that he was doing on Irish immigrants who worked for wealthy families in the Torresdale neighborhood. One of those wealthy families was named Morrell. Harry knew that I was familiar with Ned Morrell and his stepfather John Graver Johnson, both of whom were Philadelphia lawyers. Harry also mentioned that one of the Irish immigrants who worked for Morrell was named Walter Garvin. Harry was surprised that I knew Walter Garvin. Walter was a friend of my father. I was curious about the information Harry had developed.

A few weeks later, Harry sent me a first draft of his article and invited my comments. What an opportunity! I replied with a lengthy e-mail message, commenting on the time frame of the article, the customs of the Irish, some of the Northeast's Irish leaders who had not been mentioned, and my own contacts with

Walter Garvin. Harry replied, saying that after reading my comments, he decided to re-write the article – and he did. In the meanwhile, I was reading Harry's latest work, *Remembering Northeast Philadelphia.* I decided to write a commentary on some of those stories just as I did with Harry's Irish immigrant story. I would frame my commentaries in the form of letters, the way that Peter Stephen Duponceau wrote letters to his granddaughter about his experiences as a member of George Washington's staff at Valley Forge, and about practicing law in Philadelphia after the revolution.

I did not intend to send any of these letters to Harry. I knew that Harry did not have long to live. He made no secret of his affliction with cancer. I did send him an e-mail message commenting on his story about Al Schmid. I never heard back. Harry died on December 5, 2009. It was too late to engage him on the subject of his local history writings.

A few years ago, I renewed my efforts to develop my thoughts about some of Harry Silcox's stories under the general heading "Letters to Harry." It is my hope that these letters will complement the subject matter of Harry's stories and thereby add something to the recorded history of northeast Philadelphia. This is a work in progress. The following are a few of my letters.

RE: AL SCHMID

Dear Harry,

I am glad that you wrote a story about Al Schmid. He was one of my first heroes. I can still recall the stories that flew through the neighborhood about Al Schmid's bravery at Guadalcanal in 1942. On the other hand, your story focuses almost entirely on the high price he paid for his heroic deeds. Al Schmid's heroism is barely mentioned. It seems to me that the reader needs to know what Al Schmid did in order to understand the man.

The Battle of Guadalcanal was a military engagement of supreme importance. It was the United States' first offensive action in World War II, and its first major amphibious assault ever. Military theorists of that time thought that amphibious assaults were suicide. Worse yet, this amphibious assault took place in the South Pacific, more than ten thousand miles from Al's Tacony home. The Marines were equipped with weapons that were left over after the best armaments were allocated to troops in the European Theater of Operations. For Al Schmid that meant that his machine gun crew used an old .30 caliber water-cooled machine gun, not one of the newer air-cooled models. That probably did not bother Al; he was the low man on the 3-man machine gun crew. He was the ammo carrier, the "mule" who carried the heavy canisters that held belts of bullets for the machine gun. His personal weapon was a .45 caliber pistol designed in 1905 for fighting in the Philippines. Corporal Lee Diamond was in charge of the crew. PFC Johnny Rivers was the gunner. We can only imagine how Al and his buddies felt when they were told that they were going to land on the remote Island of Guadalcanal, and seize a Japanese airfield.

It is even harder to imagine how they felt a few days after the landing when the navy stopped unloading and pulled its ships back out to sea with more than half of the Marines, rations and ammunition still onboard. Al and the other Marines on the island would have to shift for themselves. They imposed a 2-meal per day restriction to stretch out their limited food supply. A large force of Japanese soldiers was sighted in the jungle, a few miles east of the Marines' position. In 1942, the Japanese were regarded as the toughest jungle fighters in the world. Al's company was moved to a defensive line on the west bank of the Ilu River (which the Marines called "Alligator Creek," thereby proving that they could not distinguish between crocodiles and alligators). Al's machine gun crew was placed in the middle of the company's defensive line.

It was just past 1:00 A.M. when suddenly, the silence was pierced by bugles, whistles and screams. Parachute flares sent ghostly shadows careening through the jungle. Explosions erupted. Incoming rifle fire tempted the Marines to retaliate and reveal their positions. The machine guns were the invaders' primary targets. There were screams and threats, "Tonight you die!" Obscure forms began to advance across the Ilu. Almost immediately, Johnny Rivers was torn in two by Japanese bullets. Corporal Diamond was hit in the shoulder and disabled. It was terrifying, an experience likely to paralyze a man with fear. Al Schmid set aside his fears, crawled up to the machine gun and took charge.

Machine gunners are taught to fire short pulsating bursts of about five rounds each in synchronization with the other machine guns along the line. That is what Al Schmid did. Even after the other machine guns were knocked out by hostile fire, Al continued to fire bursts at the attacking enemy. Rapid firing creates intense heat, a factor that increases the likelihood that the gun will jam and become inoperable. During the battle, enemy bullets ruptured the gun's water-cooling lines. The hot gun burned Al's hands but he did not let go. The gun did not jam. It was a frantic battle.

The attacks were unrelenting. Some attackers managed to get close to Schmid's machine gun but Schmid kept firing. One enemy soldier lobbed a grenade. It exploded right above the barrel of Schmid's gun. The blast hit him full front. One eye was torn apart. The other eye was blinded, and metal fragments were embedded in his face. Al was seriously wounded but he was not about to quit.

He grabbed the machine gun and resumed firing. Corporal Diamond directed the firing; he told Al when to fire higher or lower, or left or right. The fierce fight continued through the dark morning hours. The Japanese soldiers pulled back shortly before daybreak. The banks of the Ilu River were lined with the bodies of dead soldiers. The elite Japanese infantry unit was destroyed. When daylight came, Al Schmid was evacuated to a hospital ship where his wounds were treated. Meanwhile, the Battle of Guadalcanal raged on for more than four months, and involved three more major battles.

When the Marines who survived that harrowing night on the Ilu River returned to the United States, the one person that they invariably talked about was the tough kid from Company H who took charge of a machine gun and continued to operate it all night, even after being blinded by an enemy grenade. Al Schmid's initiative, courage and tenacity inspired his fellow Marines; and also inspired his neighborhood in northeast Philadelphia. Initiative, courage and tenacity, those are the qualities that Al Schmid brings to mind.

Harry, give some thought to adding these facts to your story.

Gerry

148

RE: BOULEVARD POOLS

Dear Harry,

Your story is the first I heard of alligator wrestling at Boulevard Pools. I would have thought that a story like that would have persisted forever as a part of the community folklore – like the time that Babe Ruth played for the Ascension Parish CYO baseball team in Kensington.

It is hard to imagine the owners of the pools taking such an enormous risk. If an alligator got into the crowd, he would have thought that he was at a Sunday brunch. Also, there must have been policemen or private security guards with firearms. There is no guarantee that bullets would not hit spectators. Even in 1930, the law would have held the Boulevard Pools financially liable to any injured patrons. It is interesting that there was a worker's compensation proceeding (although in 1930, it would have been called "workmen's" compensation), and a formal report of the Board. Usually, compensation is determined almost automatically unless one of the parties files an appeal to the Board. Moreover, the investors in the pools were in a good position to work out a private settlement with the Rogers brothers, particularly inasmuch as the investors were in a position to provide the Rogers brothers with jobs despite the approach of the Great Depression.

My memories of the Boulevard Pools date from about 1945 through 1950, and are sketchy at best. I went there less than a dozen times. The admission charge of $1.00 was out of my price range.

Cost aside, Boulevard Pools was impressive. It was an attractive building with Spanish style architecture, beige masonry walls and red terra cotta tile roofs. On the other hand, the interior was a disappointment. The lobby was a cold, uninviting cement room with two ticket windows on the far wall. Next to the ticket windows were two narrow metal stairways, like the ladders on a ship. Men were directed to the stairway to the left; and women went up the stairway to the right. The stairway went up approximately 30 feet, and then leveled out. There was a window to a small room where a clerk redeemed your admission ticket for a towel and a key to one of the lockers in the dressing room below. The key presented a problem. It had an elastic loop but regardless of whether you looped it on your wrist or your ankle, it interfered with your movement and was likely to come loose. Although most bathing suits had pockets, those pockets rarely retained their contents.

The doorway from the locker room to the pool had a turnstile like the subway. It assured that people entered to pool area one at a time. Over the turnstile was a garden hose that doused everyone with cold water. We tried our best to avoid that automatic shower.

One of my most persistent memories of Boulevard Pools is seeing a small group of African-Americans protesting outside the main doorway of the building. African-Americans were not allowed to enter the Boulevard Pools. It was not clear to me why they were excluded. My mother often said that the same type of exclusion was applied to people of German descent during World War I. She bore the brunt of that discrimination back in her younger days. On the other hand, the Boulevard Pools was not important in my mother's scheme of things. In approximately 1953, the Pools' racial policy changed. After it became clear that blacks would be admitted to the Pools, very few of them came. I guess it wasn't worth a dollar.

Harry, my last comment is really a question. What role did the ballroom play in the entertainment complex? I was told that it was a major forum for the big bands of the 1930s and 1940s. It was advertised as the "Boulevard Ballroom." I was only there once; and that was in the mid-1950s. The star that night was Harry James. It gave me a taste of the big band era, just as that era was dying out. Was it really a high profile place? I won't be surprised if you don't answer.

Gerry

RE: PREPARING FOR WAR:
MAYFAIR IN 1941

Dear Harry,

You ought to be ashamed of yourself. This story accuses Mayfair residents of being unpatriotic when they exercised their constitutional right to speak out against a proposed public housing project. The Mayfairs had a legitimate gripe, and they do not deserve the spin that you put on the story.

In 1941, Mayfair was an ideal residential area for working class people who were moving away from the densely populated industrial neighborhoods of Richmond, Bridesburg, Kensington and Frankford. City zoning codes offered assurance that the character of northeast Philadelphia would continue to be a low density residential area. No wonder people from the industrial neighborhoods invested their life's savings in new homes in Mayfair.

Your article is wrong when it states that the "actual cost [of a Mayfair home] was a little over $4,000." My parents bought their straight-through (not an air-light) row house on Chippendale

Avenue in March 1939. They paid $5,290. That was a lot of money for a letter carrier during the Great Depression. Corner houses on the block sold for about $7,000.

The public housing project that the city attempted to foist upon Mayfair was proposed without any real consideration of Philadelphia's zoning plans and the negative effect that the housing project would have on the residents of Mayfair. Your article suggests that the Mayfair residents had a patriotic duty to accept the decision of a city bureaucrat that a high-density housing project was necessary for "national defense." Do you remember how you characterized the high density development of the site of the Edwin Forrest Home just three blocks to the east? You said it was "sheer greed" and that the increased density made that neighborhood undesirable. In contrast to the way things were handled in the Forrest Home tract, the Mayfair homeowners did exactly what citizens are supposed to do when they have a grievance against their government. They peaceably assembled and presented their grievances – backed up by their votes. The city bureaucrats backed down.

In 1942, Congress passed the Lanham Act, which provided funds for the housing project that was the subject of your story. That housing project was built, and it was built less than two miles from the site originally proposed. The Pennypack Homes still exists as a cooperative community.

It is deserving of its own story without petty piques and neighborhood jealousies.

Harry, you can do better.

Gerry

RE: THE NAMING OF LINCOLN HIGH SCHOOL, 1949 – 1950

Dear Harry,

As Shakespeare might have said, much ado about nothing! Although naming the school after a historical person may have been a departure from the Philadelphia penchant for naming schools for the neighborhoods in which they are located, that did not prevent the next school on Cottman Avenue from being named Northeast High School.

To make matters worse, there already was a Northeast High School at Eighth and Lehigh Streets. The 8th & Lehigh school had its own academic and athletic tradition. One would think that this duplication of names might cause confusion. Not to worry! The School District simply treated the old school as a new school and the new school as an old school. They gave the "new" school at 8th & Lehigh a new name, Thomas Edison High School. The 8th & Lehigh tradition and records were carved out, and shipped up to the new – I mean the old – Northeast High School on Cottman Avenue. So much for tradition in Philadelphia schools.

By the way Harry, you misunderstood the language of Judge Kun's order dismissing Mayfair's complaint about the naming of Lincoln High. Judge Kun did not criticize "the motives of those in Mayfair who objected to the name Abraham Lincoln." Judge Kun simply said that the people who brought the suit did so on a theory that is not supported by Pennsylvania law. In other words, the law does not require that schools be named for the business or economic interests of the place where the school is located. That is why Judge Kun dismissed the complaint.

Thanks for explaining why the new and the old coexist in the Philadelphia School District.

Gerry

RE: THE "OLD" LINCOLN HIGH SCHOOL,   1950 – 2009

Dear Harry,

I was in grammar school when Abraham Lincoln High was built. The construction site was on the fields where we used to play, particularly Mayfair's athletic fields at Rowland and Ryan Avenues, and the old Poor Farm which was at the end of the cinder road that was an extension of Sheffield Avenue. To our way of thinking, it was only fair that we use the construction site as a substitute for our old playfields. As a result, I knew a good bit about the building itself, but I learned a lot from your discussion of the design objectives and the administration of its educational function. Let me share with you a few of the thoughts that occurred to me as I read this story.

First, there is the role played by the Mayfair Improvement Association. The Association owned the land along Rowland Avenue from Ryan Avenue north to about Bleigh Street, and along Ryan Avenue from Rowland west to about Sackett Street. (It was not part of Fairmount Park.) The large wooden grandstand at the corner of Rowland and Ryan was deteriorating badly and was no longer used by spectators because it was unsafe.

It would have been expensive to repair or replace the old structure. The rest of Mayfair's land was used for three baseball fields, a playground, and a toddler's wading pool that we called, "the baby pool." The caretaker of the Mayfair Improvement Association property was John Gindhart (whose cousin Joe wrote the song "On the Way to Cape May"). The Association's land was critical to the City's plans for a new high school. However, the Association was wary of the City's oral assurances of how the land would be used in the future. As you point out elsewhere in your articles, the City previously reneged on a promise to build a high school in Tacony.

Eventually, a deal was struck between the Association and the City. One of my neighbors explained the deal this way. There were two conditions. First, a high school would be built in the immediate future. Second, the residents of Mayfair would have access to the school's athletic facilities. I have not reviewed the real estate deeds for this transaction but I suspect that those documents include the terms of the deal with the Association. Interestingly, when the high school was being built, the watchman on the construction site was John Gindhart.

On another score, I am surprised that you did not mention Lincoln's 1952 Public League Champion football team. Okay, they lost the City Championship game to North Catholic. So what? I saw that game at Franklin Field. It brings back memories of Frank Slattick, Tom Tursi, Dan Fleming and other early Lincoln High athletes.

One last comment – please take a look at the last paragraph of the article. I do not understand it. It seems to say that extending the school's boundaries caused a decrease in enrollment. I suspect that you have to be a member of the Philadelphia School Board to understand that one.

Gerry

GALOOTS

One of Carl Sandburg's poems begins with the words, "Brancusi is a galoot." It is a great opening line, blunt and to the point. You don't even have to know what a galoot is; it is enough that Brancusi was one of them. Bernie Avellino was another.

As a novice lawyer in the early 1970s, I handled a number of minor accident cases defending liability insurance companies. One case was unusual. It was a very small claim. It sought only reimbursement for car rental expense while the claimant's car was being repaired, a sum of about $250. Insurance companies do not usually hire big law firms to defend such small claims. This was a fender-bender accident. A claims adjuster had already settled directly with the owner of the vehicle. My client paid the repair costs, but then the owner wanted to be reimbursed for the amount that he spent to rent a car while his car was being fixed. The insurance company refused to make any further payment on the ground that the settlement check stated that it was "the full and final settlement amount." The vehicle owner filed suit, represented by Bernard J. Avellino, one of the more aggressive personal injury lawyers in Philadelphia.

I did not know Bernie Avellino, except by reputation. My first contact with him was brief. It consisted of a phone call. Speaking in a friendly but curt tone, Bernie said, "Hey look, I would not normally handle a case like this, but I represent this guy in connection with another accident and that case involves a lot of money. So I have to pay attention to him and make him think that he was right in the way that he settled his claim. Offer me something. I'll accept it; and we will both save a lot of time and money." With that, he hung up. It was unusual, but what he said made sense. After getting approval from my client, I sent out a letter offering to settle for half the amount of the claim. A few days later, I received a letter accepting the offer, and both Avellino and I moved on to bigger and better things.

About fifteen years after that small settlement, I came across Avellino's name again. One of the local newspapers targeted Philadelphia's judiciary with a series of negative articles. In one instance, a reporter interviewed an experienced but outspoken judge who was handling criminal trials. At the close of the interview, the judge escorted the reporter to the door. There was a brief discussion about a recent trial in which a handsome young man was convicted of raping a young woman whom one of the courtroom clerks described as a "bag job." The reporter asked the judge what the clerk meant when he said that the victim was a "bag job." The judge replied that it was a term of derision. He compared it to a term that in his college days was used to describe a very unattractive female, "coyote ugly." The next morning's headlines screamed out that a Philadelphia judge described a rape victim as "coyote ugly," and Judge Bernard J. Avellino was in very hot water. In an attempt to get out of the media spotlight, he arranged to be transferred from the criminal bench to the civil trial division.

You might expect that a judge who is trying to stay out of the media spotlight would maintain a low profile. Not so Judge Avellino. Bernie was a galoot. He made it clear that he was going to reorganize the administration of the court to eliminate the inefficiency that bogged down the disposition of civil motions. His message to the civil trial bar was that he would be unpredictable, and that the rule would be "my way or the highway."

I was not sure that I wanted to be a part of the five-lawyer committee that the Bar Association appointed to work with Judge Avellino in reorganizing the filing of civil motions. It seemed to me that, as a defense lawyer, I would be the primary target of a plaintiff-oriented judge who had already signaled that he intended to run roughshod over anyone whose opinions differed from his. On the other hand, civil motions are important to all lawyers engaged in trial practice. There is no reason why the rules cannot be the same for both sides.

The members of the Bar Association committee assembled in the waiting area of Judge Avellino's City Hall chambers in advance of our first meeting. I cannot recall all of the names, but our chairman was Steve Saltz, an aggressive plaintiff's personal injury lawyer who was later elected a Legend of the Philadelphia Bar. It occurs to me that the honor of being a "Legend" is more than offset by the requirement that Legend status be granted only to those lawyers who are deceased. Bernie Smalley and Joe Fishbein, two low-key and very popular lawyers, were also on the committee. I was surprised that even the lawyers who represented plaintiffs seemed to be apprehensive about being dominated by Judge Avellino. I thought that it might be an act on their part. It was no act.

This was the first time that I met Judge Avellino face-to-face. Our only prior dealing was that telephone call and the tiny case from long ago. Now, I saw that Avellino had a distinguished appearance. He was about 50 years of age, of medium height, and had close cropped gray hair. After brief introductions, he walked behind his desk and invited us to take any of the other seats in the room. I chose an inconspicuous chair behind the others, and off to one side.

Looking at his watch, the judge announced that, since it was after 5:00 O'clock, he was going to have a scotch. Taking a crystal glass from a nearby cabinet, he poured about two fingers of whiskey into the glass and asked whether any of us would care to join him. It was an offer that none dared to accept.

In the meeting that followed, it was apparent that Judge Avellino's reputation had preceded him. Unlike previous motion court judges, Avellino did not expect practicing lawyers to participate in the development of new court rules. The development of rules was the judge's function; our role was to comment on the judge's proposals. Steve Saltz attempted to remind Judge Avellino of the long and healthy cooperation that marked the relationship of the Bar Association and the judiciary. Avellino cut him short and said that this committee would be different. He would make the rules, and we would have the opportunity to give him our comments.

The first proposed rule change highlighted the gap between the judge and the lawyers. At this late date, I forget the specifics but the proposal would have changed the procedure for handling preliminary objections. In effect, it would have given the motion court judge the discretionary power to dismiss objections at any time and for any reason. Committee members argued strenuously that the proposal was not "fair." Judge Avellino bluntly told them that he was concerned with efficiency, not fairness. Some of the committee members began to fear that continued opposition to the proposal would result in later retribution against them in future cases. You could hear it in their voices. You could see it in their eyes. Gradually, the opposition subsided.

Although I intended to keep a low profile in these committee meetings, it was clear to me that if I did not say something now, I would be hard-put to criticize the proposal at a later date. I raised my hand and suggested that Rules 1017 and

1028 of the Pennsylvania Rules of Civil Procedure prohibited the procedure that Judge Avellino wanted to adopt.

For the next ten minutes or so, the judge and I had a pointed discussion about the requirements of the Rules of Civil Procedure. It was a long time since Avellino dealt with the civil rules on a regular basis. He had been in criminal courts for about seven years. He took his rule book from the shelf, and paged along as I commented on the words of the rules in question. Eventually, he turned to me and said, "You're right!" He said that he would reconsider the subject and we would discuss it again at the next meeting.

A few weeks after the initial meeting, Steve Saltz approached me and described a procedure that he wanted me to propose to Judge Avellino. I reminded him that he was the committee chairman, and that he was the one who should speak for the committee. Steve's reply was, "You are the only one that he listens to."

Regardless of who Judge Avellino listened to, his attention was focused on the discovery filings of motion court. Everyone knew that Philadelphia's motion court was an unmitigated disaster. There were just too many cases in the system. The logistics were daunting. Each year there were nearly 45,000 civil motions filed, which in turn produced about 45,000 written responses, and 90,000 multipage briefs. The major part of these filings related to discovery. With only fifteen or so judges assigned full time to the civil trial division, several judges worked late into the night trying to keep abreast of this flood of paper. Judge Avellino told us that he had the answer.

He would eliminate the filing of written motions. Lawyers who wanted a judicial decision would phone a court clerk and obtain a date and time to present an oral motion to a judge. The appointment usually was scheduled about two weeks hence. The lawyer was then required to advise opposing counsel of the appointed time and the substance of the motion. About fifty cases were listed for each hour of court time. On the average, 42 of those 50 disputes were settled without the necessity of any court involvement at all. It was a procedure that worked in Pittsburgh, and Judge Avellino was correct in predicting that it would work in Philadelphia.

Not only did the "oral argument" system of dispute resolution clear the paper backlog of motion court filings; it also created a stage on which Judge Bernie Avellino performed twice a week. One continuing problem in resolving discovery motions involved objections to interrogatories, which sometimes numbered more than one hundred questions. Just stating each of the interrogatories was time consuming. Moreover, since most lawyers tend to use the same questions from one case to another, many of the interrogatories were irrelevant to the case at hand.

After struggling through a few mind-numbing sessions of multiple objections to multiple interrogatories, Avellino applied his flair for ingenuity and showmanship. He developed what he called "The Three Silly Questions Rule." If the lawyer objecting to the interrogatories could show that there were at least three silly questions among the interrogatories, the entire set would be stricken. Pretty soon, the other lawyers in the courtroom got into the act. After each offending question was read, Judge Avellino would look at the assembled lawyers, shrug his shoulders, and say, "You call it." In unison, the group would call, "One – Two – Three." Bernie then smiled and said "You're out!"

Avellino also applied remedies that struck fear in the hearts of some lawyers. When he took over the responsibility for motion court, he followed the practice of his predecessors that if a dispute arose at the taking of deposition testimony, the lawyers could pick up the phone and get a contemporaneous ruling from the motion court judge. On one occasion, Judge Avellino made the mistake of taking a phone call placed on a speaker-phone by a gaggle of lawyers during the course of a contentious deposition. After quickly determining that the dispute could not be handled effectively over the telephone, the judge ordered all of the lawyers to a conference in his chambers at 3:00 O'clock that afternoon.

When the conference began, the judge was told that the lawyer who initiated the phone call was not present because he was from New York and he had a ticket on the 3:30 train back to the Big Apple. Without further ado, Avellino picked up the telephone and dialed the Philadelphia Sheriff. Approximately twenty minutes later, the New York lawyer was apprehended by the sheriff's deputies at 30th Street Station. He spent the next several hours in City Hall, and eventually took a late night train home. Shortly after that experience, Judge Avellino stopped taking calls from lawyers at depositions.

In the courtroom, Avellino was like an earlier generation of judges. Unlike Pittsburgh's "Tony" Wettick, who would make his decision and then smile and call the next case, Bernie Avellino would tell the lawyers what they had done wrong, and what they could have done to make their presentation more effective. Perhaps moved by his former experience as a Philadelphia ward leader, he often encouraged female lawyers to seek election to the bench. The era for that type of judge had passed. Both judicial criticism and judicial encouragement were resented by the present generation of lawyers. When Judge Avellino was reassigned to another area of the civil trial division, younger lawyers were generally happy. However, I could not help but notice that the efficiency of the motion court declined. Not every judge has the skills necessary to rule immediately after an oral presentation. Not everyone is a galoot.

For all of his judicial ability, Bernie Avellino seemed to have a death wish. In my more than 40 years in the practice of trial law, I tried to separate myself from the internal politics of the judiciary. That world is not a part of my concern. On the other hand, it is a world that everyone knows exists. A lawyer who once was a ward leader and a force in local politics is not likely to change his stripes when elected to the bench. Undoubtedly, some judges are happy to get out of the political fray; but for others, the competition just moves to another level. Bernie Avellino was one of those judges who carried politics to another level. Unfortunately, Bernie lost sight of the fact that his actions reflected not just on himself, but on the judiciary of Pennsylvania as a whole. He refused to perform assignments that he considered to be personally demeaning. After the Supreme Court of Pennsylvania told him in no uncertain terms to get back to work, he retired from the bench.

Bernie Avellino retired to his summer home in Ocean City, New Jersey. One afternoon in November 2000, he was watching TV in his living room when he dropped off to sleep. He never woke up. His heart simply stopped beating, and did not restart.

I drove down to Ocean City for the funeral Mass at St. Augustine's Church, around the block from the 14th Street beach. It was a long time since I had been in Ocean City. The trip took a bit longer than expected. I arrived just at the beginning of the Mass. My eyesight was deteriorating, and I could not immediately identify the mourners in the church. The faces of the people on the altar blended together. I took a seat near the back of the church. The homily was not what I expected. The voice of the priest was right out of South Philadelphia. The subject matter was not Bernie the Judge, but Bernie the Ward Leader; the ward leader who knows the neighborhood and takes care of his flock; the ward leader who gets them jobs; who gets them food and fuel supplements. It was the ward leader who guided them through the rocks and shoals of city regulations.

The voice sounded like one of Philadelphia's ward leaders. I was reminded of Tom Guenther, one of my classmates from St. Joseph's College, who worked as a labor union representative and also as a political intern before entering the seminary in Camden. Tom was a piece of work. I last saw him at the Reading Terminal Market. It was Christmastime, and the

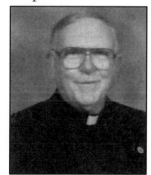

REV.MONSIGNOR
THOMAS A GUENTHER

market was crowded with shoppers. As soon as I heard my name ring out above the noise of the crowd, I knew who it was. Tom was wearing an old black windbreaker. He looked for all the world like a longshoreman. Before that, it was at a political rally for Bob Casey at the old Palumbo's Restaurant. We were both sitting at a table with Mike and Fay Stack. You never knew where Tom Guenther would show up.

At the end of Bernie Avellino's funeral Mass, the congregation filtered through the doors at the back of the church where we were greeted by the celebrant, Reverend Monsignor Thomas A. Guenther. It was a two-galoot funeral.

THE RAINMAKERS

One of the more interesting terms used in the practice of law is "rainmaker." Invariably, when I hear the word rainmaker I think of Corporal James Tafoya, a full-blooded Shoshone Paiute American Indian, doing an energetic dance and imploring those "damned California rain gods" to dampen down the terrain at Camp Pendleton. The California rain gods paid little or no attention to Jimmy Tafoya; maybe they didn't like people from the Four Corners area of Colorado. Then again, maybe Tafoya was not a rainmaker. In the practice of law, a rainmaker is a lawyer who brings profitable business to the law firm. Some lawyers are rainmakers and some are not.

In 1969, when I joined the Firm of Schnader, Harrison, Segal and Lewis in Philadelphia, Bernie Segal was a consummate rainmaker. Clients that Bernie brought into the firm accounted for about one-half of the firm's gross revenues. How did Bernie come to be a rainmaker? That is an interesting question.

Bernard G. Segal finished first in his class at the Law School of the University of Pennsylvania in 1931. He was brilliant. The Dean of the Law School referred Bernie to Pennsylvania Attorney General William A. Schnader, who needed someone to draft a comprehensive banking code. Schnader and Segal were two of a kind, albeit separated by about twenty years in age. Both were devoted to the law and both were workaholics. At the end of Schnader's term as attorney general, he lost a close election for Governor of Pennsylvania and returned to Philadelphia and the private practice of law. Segal joined his boss in the new 3-man firm and benefited from Schnader's business contacts and his connections with influential organizations such as the American Law Institute and the National Association of Commissioners on Uniform Laws. Four years later, when Schnader suffered a massive stroke while arguing a case in the Supreme Court of Pennsylvania, Segal took the lead in representing the firm's major clients.

Bernie Segal had an instinctive ability to ingratiate himself with people. It was almost second nature to him. He knew the names of the clients' children and often was in a position to assist those children in being admitted to prestigious schools. He was close to the leaders of the medical community and could recommend doctors to clients and assist them in getting preferential medical appointments. When he undertook the representation of a new client, such as the department store delivery company United Parcel Service, he quickly became close friends with its top executives. Similarly, he exerted his leadership in the bar associations. In 1952, he was elected Chancellor of the Philadelphia Bar Association, the first Jew to hold that office. When his term as Chancellor ended, he served as the Philadelphia Bar's representative to the American Bar Association, where he convinced the Eisenhower administration to allow the ABA to comment on the qualifications of judicial nominees. His committee did an outstanding job reviewing the qualifications of those nominees and, in the process, Bernie Segal got to know virtually every federal judge in the country. He was elected president of the ABA. Hardly a day would go by when Bernie did not receive a phone call from a member of the Supreme Court of the United States. In the legal community, Bernie Segal had clout. He was the kind of lawyer that important people want to represent them.

It did not hurt that Bernie had highly qualified lawyers associated with him. For example, many Philadelphia lawyers think that Bernie's younger brother, Irving R. ("Buddy") Segal, was brighter and a more effective advocate than Bernie. Buddy exceeded all of Bernie's academic records at the University of Pennsylvania. When UPS wanted someone to handle the exhaustive administrative trials that would allow UPS to compete against parcel post, Bernie made the arrangements with the client and then assigned Buddy to handle those impossible trials. (Buddy won those cases.) Similarly, when John B. King, general counsel of The Bell Telephone Company of Pennsylvania, wanted a trial lawyer to represent Bell in a rate investigation being conducted by the Public Utility Commission, Bernie assigned Buddy to that task and later backed him up with George P. Williams, III, another top-flight trial lawyer. Again the representation was successful. But Buddy Segal was not a rainmaker. Buddy was recognized as an outstanding trial and appellate lawyer, but he did not bring many clients to the firm.

Even Buddy's work for Bell Telephone waxed and waned despite his successes for that client. Someone told Buddy that this was due to one of Bell's officers whose wife valued the Main Line social connections of a lawyer from another firm. Maybe that lawyer's blue-blood background made him a rainmaker.

In the 1980s, the telephone industry was beset with a technological revolution that brought about the dismantling of the old Bell System. The plan called for Bell of Pennsylvania to be phased out in favor of a regional company, Bell Atlantic, which later became Verizon. The Pennsylvania Public Utility Commission seized the opportunity to conduct a broad investigation of the entire telephone industry. Buddy and I, along with Bob Kendall, represented AT&T Communications of Pennsylvania in that generic investigation. We did a good job. All regulatory restraints on AT&T were removed. In retrospect, we did too good a job. With no regulatory oversight, AT&T no longer needed outside trial lawyers.

Still, there was a place for rainmakers in the ever-changing world of law. Frequently, lawyers with profitable client bases sought out other law firms that might increase their personal compensation. For the most part, these were not rainmakers in the sense that Bernie Segal was a rainmaker. Most of these lawyers were what my old friend Bob Boger used to call, "little big-shots." They talked about "portable business," bringing to mind the image of a camel caravan crossing the wastelands of the Middle East. Somehow, the term rainmaker does not comport with the mental picture of camels and arid wastelands. Suffice it to say that there are still lawyers who are highly skilled, and who have clout in the legal community.

In the meanwhile, Bell's successor, Verizon, was in the news last week. It occurred during the criminal trial of Senator Vincent Fumo, a lawyer and powerful Pennsylvania legislator. Fumo was a significant force behind an effort by Pennsylvania lawmakers to break up the corporate organization of Verizon, a move that, if successful, could cost the company billions of dollars. Verizon's president testified to the effect that, he was told by Fumo that if Verizon spent $50 million for the expenses specified on a list presented to him by Fumo, the legislative effort to break up the company would be abandoned.

Interestingly, two of the items on the senator's list involved law firms. One would have required Verizon to retain a law firm with which Fumo was previously associated and to spend at least $500,000 on that legal work. Another item would have required Verizon to spend at least $3 million on legal work done by another law firm, a firm led by one of Fumo's close friends. News commentators castigated Vince Fumo for using his elected office to extort benefits for himself and his friends. The opinion media argued that Fumo's tactics were unethical, immoral and even criminal. What was Senator Fumo's defense to these charges? He said that everything he did was above board and consistent with accepted legal tradition. He was just a rainmaker.

In my mind's eye I can see Bernie Segal's enigmatic smile.

BINK HAVILAND

Your given name may be Bancroft, but to us you were simply "Bink." What a great name for someone who wore a perpetual smile.

When you arrived at 1719 Packard Building in the early hours of the morning, you had that "rumpled" look as though you had already worked a full eight hours. At lunchtime, you had not changed one bit; you still looked exactly the same. By 6:00 p.m., that rumpled look was understandable but there was no perceptible difference from the way you looked hours earlier. Depositions often continued into the evening hours at an unperturbed pace. As the hour grew later, you prefaced your questions with, "I am cognizant of the late hour but ...." There was no limit to your quiet energy.

Maybe that persistent energy is why the firm often assigned you to cases that required tenacity over long periods of time. I can still recall your report to our Litigation Committee on a case in which you sought to enforce a motion picture copyright, and you pursued the film pirate through a chain of courts that stretched from the Pocono Mountains into northern New Jersey. Actually, the written minutes of that meeting were more interesting than the oral report that you presented.

The movie was *"The Naked Lady,"* and the minutes described how you pursued the Naked Lady from the back woods of Eaglesmere, Pennsylvania through neighboring New Jersey – never once mentioning that the Naked Lady was a movie. It sounded like a James Bond story. To obtain a restraining order for the Naked Lady, you presented an emergency petition to a New Jersey judge who happened to be attending a wedding reception at a suburban country club. And so it went, for several exciting paragraphs. You got the restraining order, but I forget what became of the Naked Lady.

Remember the case against Dow Chemical? The case surfaced on the eve of Thanksgiving Day, and required emergency action over the holiday weekend. We must have spoiled Judge John Lord's Thanksgiving because he entered a case management order that ruined our Christmas and New Year's holidays. Critical depositions of Dow's officers were scheduled to begin at the company's headquarters in Midland, Michigan on December 16th, and my wife was expecting our third child on that same day. I can still see you at the airport boarding a plane for Michigan. You really expected me to go with you. Today I told that story to my daughter Sharon. She laughed.

Over the years, most of our conversations were about family, soccer, the Westtown School, and your island retreat in Canada. It is a common recollection of you shared by many lawyers in our firm. On occasion, we talked about another island.

I wonder how many of your Quaker clan know that you participated in the Battle of Okinawa?

INCENSE AND NONSENSE

Today is the Feast of the Epiphany. Probably that is why the monsignor called for a censer and wafted incense over the altar, an unusual occurrence during an ordinary Sunday Mass. I have no great appreciation for things liturgical, but the pungent odor of incense invariably takes me back to 1719 Packard Building in Philadelphia.

We had just entered Buddy Segal's office at the far end of the 17th floor. Buddy and George Williams were senior partners in the law firm and both were dominating personalities. Buddy had a brilliant, incisive mind, a flair for the dramatic, and the ability instantaneously to shift his personality from gregarious to hostile, and vice versa. George was tall and rangy, with a booming baritone voice and an irrepressible sense of humor. Buddy, George and I often worked together on matters for UPS and for The Bell Telephone Company of Pennsylvania. On this particular occasion, I suspect that we came together to discuss a UPS matter because Bill Barnes was with us. Bill was then a mid-level partner who spent a lot of time on UPS cases. Hardly had we entered Buddy's office when Bill said that he detected an unusual odor in the room.

I did not notice anything unusual, but I was not about to comment on the status of Buddy Segal's office. Buddy and Bill went sniffing around the room. George and I looked on in silence. Soon, Bill stopped in front of a dried-out plant near the window. Pointing to the plant, Bill said, "This is where it is coming from. It smells like incense." Without any hesitation, George Williams bellowed, "It is only appropriate that there be incense in a shrine!" George then doubled up in laughter at his own comment.

George made that comment more than thirty-five years ago, but it still comes to mind every time I see a priest swing a censer back and forth. I think of George and Buddy; and I smile.

PERRY S. BECHTLE

It hardly seems like yesterday – much less 35 years – since that day you came to my office to discuss a very sensitive case that directly involved a member of your law firm. Your reputation preceded you. I was told that you were one of the best lawyers in Philadelphia, a credit to the bar. You certainly lived up to your advance billing. After an enjoyable conversation, we settled that case to the satisfaction of both our clients. And true to your word, you promptly returned the book that you borrowed from me, the one about the New York law firm of Hummel & Howe. It was not one of your most important cases. You probably forgot about it years ago. But for me, it was a memorable event.

I never mentioned it to you, but a few years after our settlement discussion I had the opportunity to view a videotape that you made for the lawyers in the Office of the City Solicitor. It was about the way you handled difficult cases. You said that you started by ingratiating yourself with opposing counsel. "I always go to the other lawyer's office. It shows them that I am comfortable on their turf." You also said that you try to establish a personal bond. "I will often borrow a book from them." I cannot recall too much of the tape after that point. I was laughing too hard.

You were a classic Philadelphia lawyer. Ave atque vale!

FAR FROM THE TREE

It is a common expression: "the fruit fell far from the tree." It refers to children who are far different from their parents. This Isaac Newton-like expression occurred to me during the funeral Mass for Judge Lisa Aversa Richette.

Lisa was a piece of work. She was one-of-a-kind, an original. In 1952, when I was completing my sophomore year of high school, Lisa Aversa graduated from Yale Law School. There were only four other women in her graduating class. It was tough

for women to succeed in the legal profession in those days. Lisa accepted the challenge. She became an assistant district attorney, one of the few jobs open to women lawyers at that time. She wrote an authoritative text about social justice for children. Eventually she was elected a judge of the Court of Common Pleas of Philadelphia. Her long black hair, slender build and penchant for dangling jewelry made Judge Richette a natural target for political cartoonists. On the bench, she was well known for her compassion and her strong support for women and children, regardless of whether they were the victims or the persons accused of crimes. Often, her decisions were not popular. Former mayor (and police commissioner) Frank Rizzo, called her "Let 'em loose Lisa."

I met Lisa Richette in 1990 when Bart Sheehan persuaded me to attend a retreat for lawyers at the old Jesuit retreat house, Manresa, across the Severn River from the Naval Academy. The retreat was to be directed by Robert F. Drinan, SJ, who had once been a significant member of Congress. I was unable to persuade any other lawyers from Philadelphia to accompany me to the retreat. It was late when I arrived at Manresa on a Friday evening. I was told that there might still be some food available in the kitchen. It was good advice. The cook had left several pieces of fish warming on the stove and there was a full pot of hot coffee. A gray haired man and a woman were talking at one of the tables. The woman was in her early sixties. She reminded me of Philadelphia's Judge Richette but her hairstyle was different and, based on her reputation in the news media, I did not expect to find Judge Richette at a Jesuit retreat. She smiled, walked over to me and said, "Hello, my name is Lisa Richette."

Over the next few days, I learned a lot about Lisa Richette. She was a student of religion. She regularly attended retreats, and was even qualified to direct retreats herself. She knew most of the Jesuits at Manresa and considered one of them to be her personal chaplain. Lisa was also active in charitable activities in Philadelphia, particularly charities that helped women and those that assisted victims of AIDS. She was very different from the person who was presented in the newspapers. In 1993, I nominated Lisa Richette as a candidate for the Saint Thomas More Award, which is presented annually to a member of the Catholic legal community who represents the principles and ideals of St. Thomas More. The nomination was approved and the award was presented at a dinner following the Red Mass in October 1993. It was in making arrangements for the award dinner that I learned about Lisa's son.

Lisa introduced Laurence Richette at the award dinner as "a doctoral candidate in history at the University of Pennsylvania and also a writer and novelist." Lawyers who had known Lisa for years described Laurence as "a troubled young man." Over the years following that award dinner, I frequently heard stories of the troubles of Laurence Richette. He was a loner. People who knew him said that he was "strange." Mental illness was often suggested as a reason for his behavior. Undoubtedly, mental illness played a part in the recent series of events including a physical attack and beating of the 79-year old Lisa Richette by her son Laurence. Lisa told the District Attorney that she would not testify against her son. She died from lung cancer before the preliminary hearing was held. The fruit fell far from the tree.

JOE EGAN

In 1964, you were a part of the Redevelopment Authority's "Old Real Estate" crowd — people without college degrees who had been the backbone of many real estate offices throughout the City. Members of the old crowd were title clerks, conveyancers, deed specialists, appraisers and salesmen. They all knew each other.

You were not old but you did have several years experience with the Castor Avenue real estate office of Democratic City Committee Secretary John F. Byrne. That was where you learned about commercial real estate transactions. You proudly proclaimed that you did not use John Byrne's political clout to get your job at the Authority. "If he knew I wanted to leave his office, he surely would have blocked me from getting this job." Later, you learned that Byrne personally approved each new employee of the Authority, you included. Oh well, no one said that you were always right!

In those days, you often took the lead in organizing parties for the real estate crowd. Also, you helped carry Joe Gindhart's piano out of the house and into the back yard where he would play his song, "On the Way to Cape May." Those were comfortable times.

Remember the one-on-one basketball games that we played on weekends and at lunch? You were contentious; you always went right for the basket. After the games, you would claim that you won. I knew better. We joked about that for years.

Your work style was exactly like your basketball style, outspoken – in-your-face. You always spoke your mind. It drove your boss Ed Kick to distraction. When the newly elected Rizzo administration made Ben Rudzinski the scapegoat for all that they perceived to be wrong with City Hall, you were the only one to stand up and defend Ben by stating the facts of the case. You didn't forget your friends under the stress of political pressure.

I was surprised when you threw your hat in the political ring and ran for mayor back in 1991. Walt D'Alessio said it best, "Running for election to the office of Mayor of Philadelphia is like trying to break *into* jail!"

We last saw each other crossing Market Street at 16th. At first, I did not recognize the guy with the white hair but the big smile was a dead give-away. You muttered something about a one-on-one basketball game – but you got the ending wrong. Some things never change. And some things and some people we never forget.

A TALE OF TWO MOVIES

Normally, an e-mail message about a movie would not peak my interest. But this e-mail was an exception. It was about the movie "Letters from Iwo Jima." The message brought to mind a mental picture of Philadelphia lawyer Jim McEldrew, one of the few people I knew who fought in the Battle of Iwo Jima. He was only nineteen years old at the time, fresh out of West Catholic High School, when he found himself on the slopes of Mt. Suribachi, on a heavily fortified volcanic island in the Pacific Ocean. More than 6,800 Americans died on that island, and another 19,000 were wounded in the fighting. Jim was lucky to have survived the battle. He was not inclined to talk about his experience on Iwo but when told about a television documentary in which Japanese and American survivors of the battle concluded the show by shaking hands, Jim could not restrain himself. He blurted out, *"I wouldn't have shaken hands with those bastards."*

The movie "Letters from Iwo Jima" presents a story of the battle from a Japanese perspective. It is a counterpoint to the movie "Flags of Our Fathers," which tells the story of the flag-raisers in the famous Iwo Jima photograph. In the "Letters" movie, the Japanese soldiers are portrayed as a mirror image of their American adversaries, displaying not only bravery but also a deep concern for their families back home and, in one instance, sharing their scarce medicine supply with a mortally wounded U.S.

Marine. The main theme of the show seems to be that there was little difference between the combatants on opposite sides of the battle. "Don't you believe it!" was the point of the e-mail message I received.

The message was sent by Professor Emeritus Lester Tenney of Arizona State University, a survivor of the Bataan Death March. Professor Tenney argues that the well-documented record of atrocities committed by Japanese soldiers, including rape, decapitation, murder, setting prisoners on fire, and using them for bayonet practice, fly in the face of the movie's theme. Tenney saw no Japanese "nice guys" on the Bataan peninsula.

Tenney's message reminds me of Joe Geib's reaction when I told him that Japan was the highlight of my tour of duty in the Far East. Reverend Joseph M. Geib, SJ, was the Dean of Men, i.e., the disciplinarian, at St. Joseph's College in Philadelphia. In the late 1930s, he was in Manila. When the war broke out, many Filipinos kept him apprised of the barbarity of the invading Japanese soldiers. For Joe Geib, there was no question about it; the Japanese were barbarians. Father Geib found it difficult to understand my admiration for the Japanese people that I met in 1962.

My first contact with Japan occurred in April 1962, when I was part of an advance party of the 3rd Battalion, 3rd Marines, landing on Numazu Beach and making preparations for the battalion quarters at the base of Mt. Fuji. A Japanese army officer who accompanied us was pretty much my mirror image. He too was about six feet tall, 190 pounds and he and I had exactly the same haircut. We got along very well.

A few weeks later, when I had the opportunity to visit Tokyo, I came into contact with many Japanese who were not a part of the military. Typically, that contact came in one of Tokyo's many parks and gardens. These people were well dressed, some of them in American-style suits and some of them wearing traditional Japanese kimonos. By and large, they had a dignified bearing. Although they were not hostile, they did not go out of their way to make our acquaintance. Suffice it to say that the Japanese people with whom I came into contact favorably impressed me. My contact with Japan ended in 1963, when I mustered out of the service, returned to Philadelphia.

By the late 1970s, I was a civil trial lawyer. One of my clients manufactured power lawnmowers. In approximately 1980, a case against the manufacturer was assigned to trial in Philadelphia before Judge William M. Marutani and a jury. Judge Marutani was a native of the State of Washington. His parents were immigrants from Japan. At the age of 19-years, along with his family, Marutani was incarcerated in a government internment facility at Tule Lake, California. Later, he earned a commission in the U.S. Army and served in the Nisei Regiment during the latter phase of the Second World War. During the trial of the lawnmower case, Judge Marutani and I struck up a friendly relationship that continued after the case was settled.

When Judge Marutani retired from the bench, he moved to nearby Media, Pennsylvania, and we often saw each other on the 69th Street elevated and on the Media trolley. During those trolley rides, it was clear to me that Bill Marutani was proud of his Japanese heritage. He was a nationally recognized spokesman for the Japanese American community. President Carter appointed him to the Commission on Wartime Relocation and Internment of Civilians. More to the point, he was much like the people whom I had met and admired in Japan.

I thought of Bill Marutani when an Internet search led me to the text of a presentation made by Dr. James C. McNaughton to a 1994 Conference of Army Historians. McNaughton suggested that the activities of the Nisei Regiment constitute a relatively untapped source of data that could shed light on the racial hatred that ran deep in the Pacific War. Some members of the Nisei Regiment were school classmates of the Japanese soldiers that they interrogated in the Pacific. How could the conduct of classmates have been so different? The consensus seems to be that, after the First World War, the Japanese military adopted the view that the Japanese were the "chosen people," that their emperor was a deity and that people of other nations were less than human. Accordingly, it did not matter how those subhumans were treated or mistreated. Anything was permissible.

The emperor did nothing to change that outlook. Accordingly, in the view of the average Japanese soldier, savage conduct seemed to have imperial sanction.

Some Internet stories attempted to equalize the batting averages on atrocities by suggesting that the American firebomb raids on Tokyo and the atom bombs dropped on Hiroshima and Nagasaki were atrocities equivalent to those of the Japanese during the war. Other commentators focused on instances of Americans mutilating the corpses of dead Japanese soldiers, and argued that these occurrences were the equivalent of Nanking, Bataan and the death camps to which prisoners of war were sent.

Back in Camp Pendleton in 1960, Sergeant Butler had a few black and white photographs that were taken during the Korean War. The photos showed a younger Butler standing next to the bodies of uniformed North Korean soldiers who had so many holes in them that they looked like Swiss cheese. Butler said that, after a battle, someone emptied a full clip of B.A.R. ammo into the dead body and that one of the Marines who had a camera charged a dollar or two to take pictures of his buddies standing next to the riddled body. "There is always someone who has a camera." In a way, it was like those photos that you see of big game hunters standing next to their kill. It was a grisly souvenir but it was a far cry from the photos that I have seen of Japanese soldiers decapitating prisoners with swords, or conducting bayonet practice against prisoners whose hands and feet were tied.

Worse yet were the dismal survival rates of the prisoners in the Japanese P.O.W. camps.

No doubt the Hollywood moviemakers viewed themselves as being profound when they showed the opposing forces on Iwo Jima as mirror images of each other. But they achieved that profound result by closing their eyes to the cold, hard facts. The Japanese survivors of Iwo Jima were not subjected to a death march. The Japanese survivors of Iwo Jima were not brutalized for the enjoyment of the victors. Apparently, the moviemakers did not know how to deal with an indisputable record of criminal atrocities in the context of otherwise comparable peoples. I wonder whether it occurred to them to study how historians in other parts of the world dealt with such atrocities. Aleksandr Solzhenitsyn dealt with similar issues in his masterpiece, *The Gulag Archipelago*. Solzhenitsyn put it this way:

> "If only there were evil people somewhere
> insidiously committing evil deeds, and it were
> necessary only to separate them from the rest of
> us and destroy them. But the line dividing good
> and evil cuts through the heart of every human
> being."

Unfortunately, some moviemakers erase the line dividing good and evil. To them it is irrelevant. It gets in the way of their story. But the line dividing good and evil will not go away.

Maybe that line should be drawn in the sands of Iwo Jima. And when that line is drawn, put me on the side of Jim McEldrew.

AUS HOGAN

The obituary in *The Philadelphia Daily News* described Austin Hogan as "A Highly Regarded Products Liability Lawyer." The Aus Hogan that I knew was a whole lot more than just a "products liability lawyer." As a public defender, Austin tried a lot of criminal cases. Later, he handled an antitrust suit against my firm's client American Express Company. Aus was one of those old-time lawyers who handled any type of case that came down the pike.

I rarely had any courtroom contact with Austin Hogan. More likely, I would see him on Chestnut Street, walking down the sidewalk with his brief case in his hand, and looking up at the tall buildings.

"Hey Austin, what are you looking for?"

"Happiness."

My memories of Aus are mainly those from Mayfair, St. Matt's grammar school, and St. Joseph's College. We were in the same class in college. I made sure that the Class of 1959 received a copy of Aus' obit by e-mail. Austin's obituary drew a substantial response. One memory predominated. In our junior year of college, the class presented a minstrel show. Austin's contribution to the show was to write and sing a ditty that was in keeping with the calypso songs of those times. He called it "The Original Sin Mambo." It went like this:

> "Original Sin, Original Sin,
> Everybody's born with Original Sin;
> Whether you're fat,
> Or whether you're thin,
> You just can't win with Original Sin.
> "According to the Council of Trent,
> Everybody's born with an evil bent;
> In the hole before you begin,
> And all because of Original Sin."

It is now fifty-five years after the fact, and our classmates still remember the tune and most of them remember the words.

The Interlocutor of that minstrel show was Ed Connolly, who is now a priest in charge of two parishes in the hard-scrabble town of Girardville, Pennsylvania. Father Ed made this response to the obituary:

> "Aus was smarter than any human being has a right to be,
> But he carried it with such grace and good humor!
> Whenever I was in Austin's company,
> I came away happier for it!
> Not a bad epitaph!"

Factoring Companies Thwart the Aims of the Structured Settlement Protection Act

Once there was widespread acceptance, even enthusiasm, for structured settlements. Structured settlements involve annuity contracts by which all or part of a personal injury settlement is paid out at future intervals and includes additional amounts attributable to the earnings achieved during the life of the deferred payout. Section 104(a) of the Internal Revenue Code provides that the entire amount of those future annuity payments is non-taxable income. Structured settlements are especially advantageous when the recipient of the settlement is a minor or a person who is unable to manage his or her assets.

Consider the case of a young man whom I will call Rodger. In 1997, when he was 18 years old, Rodger was injured in an automobile accident. The injury had a settlement value of about $75,000. Rodger did not have the organizational or financial skills to manage large sums of money. Rodger's parents feared that he would dissipate the entire settlement amount before the year was out. They thought they had the answer when their lawyer negotiated a structured settlement that called for:

1. $25,000 cash at the execution of the settlement agreement;

2. $ 7,150 payable in year three;

3. $10,000 payable in year six;

4. $15,000 payable in year nine;

5. $20,000 payable in year twelve; and

6. $30,000 payable in year fifteen.

Thus, Rodger had cash-in-hand that he could invest and that would enable him to afford further schooling or job training. Moreover, he was assured that a major part of the settlement money would be available to him when he reached his mid-30s and was likely to have a family and additional responsibilities.

The insurance company paid Rodger $25,000 in cash and purchased an annuity for him with the remaining $50,000. Over the life of the settlement, Rodger was to receive a total of $107,150.00. It was a "win-win" situation. But the best laid plans of lawyers oft go astray. Law sometimes develops in accordance with Newton's third law of motion, "for every action there is an equal and opposite reaction." In the case of structured settlements, the opposite reaction was the evolution of factoring companies that prey on the same human weaknesses that structured settlements were intended to overcome. The factoring companies appeal directly to the beneficiaries' subjective need for immediate gratification and they buy out future annuity payments at sub-bargain-basement prices. Or as one such company advertises, they turn future payments into Cash Now!

In 2000, the Pennsylvania Legislature, along with the legislatures of many other states throughout the country, attempted to address these factoring practices through the Structured Settlement Protection Act, 40 Pa. C.S. §§ 4001 *et seq.* In essence, the Act requires that every buy out of structured settlement payment rights be approved by the court. Further, the court must determine that the payee has been provided with the disclosure information required by the Act, and that "the transfer is in the best interests of the payee or his dependents." 40 Pa. C.S. § 4003(a)(3). Experience with this legislation shows serious deficiencies that require judicial attention.

The Structured Settlement Protection Act does not specify how a court should go about determining that a transfer of structured settlement payment rights is in the best interests of the payee or his dependents. Some courts seem to treat the payee's testimony as determinative of the issue. Other courts exercise an increased level of judicial discretion. For example, in *In re Macumber (321 Henderson Receivables)*, 66 Pa. D&C4th 249 (Monroe Cty. 2003), where petitioner sought to transfer the right to payments that would total $17,250 in return for a cash payment of $9,521.90, the court determined that the transfer clearly was not in the best interest of the payee, stating (66 Pa.D&C4th at 252):

"The discount rate being charged by 321 Henderson Receivables Limited Partnership [the factoring company] is in excess of any interest rate allowed under Pennsylvania law and the payee did not give any coherent or rational reasons for entering such a bad bargain at this time."

Similarly, in *In re Curto (321 Henderson Receivables)*, 67 Pa. D&C4th 65 (Phila. Cty. 2004), where a 20-year-old man sought to transfer an annuity having a present value of $38,627 for a cash payment of $25,000, Judge Gene D. Cohen analogized the function of the court in determining the best interests of the payee to the court's function in scrutinizing matters affecting the rights of incompetents and its function in reviewing and approving commutation of worker's compensation benefits. Judge Cohen arrived "at the inescapable conclusion that the petitioner may have a disability and is an individual living on the margins of existence [but] it would be hazardous to his future now to entrust him with a lump sum payment . . . ." (67 Pa. D&C4th at 71).

It was inevitable that Rodger would come into contact with one of the factoring companies. He found it on the Internet. It was during the month of July, about sixty days after he received the third annuity payment, in the amount of $10,000. The factoring company was interested in buying the next two annuity payments—the fourth payment of $15,000 and the fifth payment of $20,000—a total purchase of $35,000. The discounted present value of those payments was $28,297.57. The factor offered to buy those payments for the total sum of $18,000, less costs of approximately $400, a net sale price of $17,600. Also, the factor insisted that Rodger contact an attorney to advise him in the transaction. The lawyer's fee was a flat $1,250, plus costs of about $275, a total of $1,525. The lawyer's fee and costs would be deducted from the cash payment, leaving Rodger with a net amount of $16,075. Some observers view it as a $16,075 loan in return for a guaranteed payment of $35,000. Rodger's petition for approval of the transfer stated that he planned to use the funds to start a small business and to pay off child-support arrearages of approximately $1,200. The court conducted a hearing. Rodger was the only witness. Following Rodger's testimony, the court entered an order in the form submitted by Rodger's lawyer, finding that "the best interests of the Payee, taking into account the welfare and support of the Payee's dependents, render the transfer appropriate." Within one month of the court's approval, the money was gone.

Rodger withdrew most of the money from his bank account in increments that were in the $100 to $200 range. Rodger made withdrawals from ATMs as often as five times in a single day. His child-support obligations continue to be in arrears. Rodger did not intend this result; he was simply unable to control it. By the time Rodger's family learned about the transfer, it was too late. The appeal period had expired. The statutory disclosures had been given. The court had approved the sale. The structure was undone.

The deconstruction of Rodger's structured settlement is troubling, especially in light of the Structured Settlement Protection Act's requirement that a court determine "that the transfer is in the best interests of the payee or his dependents." There is no available transcript of Rodger's hearing but after examining the court record and the few papers that Rodger managed to keep, one wonders whether the court made any inquiry at the hearing with respect to:

1. **The reason why the annuity was created in the first instance.** Farmers have a saying that you should never tear down a fence without first finding out why it was put up. A phone call or a written inquiry to the lawyer who negotiated the settlement, or to Rodger's parents, would have disclosed to the court Rodger's inability to manage his financial affairs. Simply giving notice of the hearing to the parents and the lawyer who negotiated the structure also might have had the effect of informing the court of Rodger's disability. But the Act does not require that notice of the petition be given to the persons who created the annuity.

2. **The reason why Rodger's child-support obligations were in arrears so soon after he received a non-taxable payment in the amount of $10,000.** The support order was issued by the same court that approved the sale of the annuity payments. Those facts were available to the court in its computer database. Rodger's failure to manage his annuity payments was obvious on the face of the petition. It is surprising that the court missed it.

3. **The failure to give notice of the hearing to the mother of Rodger's child.** "Dependents" is defined in the Structured Settlement Protection Act as including "payee's minor children . . . and other persons for whom the payee is legally obligated to provide support." (40 Pa.C.S. § 4002.) With a support order in place and the payments in arrears, the transfer of rights to the fourth and fifth payments clearly affected Rodger's child. The Structured Settlement Protection Act does not require, however, that notice be given to anyone except the annuity issuer and the structured settlement obligor—in most cases, the same entity. Should not the court be informed of the interests of petitioner's dependents? Should not the court-ordered recipient of child-support payments have the opportunity to oppose the wasting of assets? The court must be informed of the circumstances of petitioner's dependents if the court is to make a determination that a sale of future payments is in their best interests. In other cases, there may be other areas of inquiry that would be helpful to the court in making its determinations as to the payee's best interests. There is an excellent article on the subject in the ABA publication *The Judges' Journal*, volume 44, no. 2, Spring 2005, titled "Transfers of Structured Settlement Payment Rights: What Judges Should Know About Structured Settlement Protection Acts," by Daniel W. Hindert and Craig H. Ulman.

In Rodger's case, the function of his attorney is also troubling. The factoring company's documents refer to the attorney as an "advisor." The Structured Settlement Protection

Act requires the court to determine that "the payee has received or expressly waived in a separate written acknowledgment signed by the payee, *independent legal advice regarding the implications of the transfer* . . . ." (40 Pa.C.S. § 4003(a)(4), emphasis added.)

Rodger's attorney, after reviewing the facts of the matter, advised Rodger not to go forward with such a bad deal. He gave that advice knowing that, in all likelihood, his fees would not be paid if Rodger followed that advice and canceled the sale. But Rodger wanted "Cash Now." Factors have a way with words. Accordingly, the attorney's role became that of an advocate who undertakes to guide the client's case through the rocks and shoals of a court hearing without regard to the attorney's personal view of the transaction. One cannot criticize the attorney for not serving the child's mother with notice of the petition when the law does not require such notice. The fault—if fault there be—lies in the statute itself, which does not require that interested parties be notified of the hearing, does not require that the factoring companies be parties to the court proceeding, and thereby gives the impression that transfers ought to be approved so long as the objective requirements of the Act are satisfied.

In the meanwhile, beneficiaries of structured settlements must look to the court to provide the equal and opposite reaction that is needed to achieve the purposes of the Structured Settlement Protection Act.

BY THE NUMBERS

Suppose you are offered a contract to work full time for thirty consecutive days. The only open item is the amount of your compensation. You have two compensation choices: (1) a lump sum amount of $300,000, or (2) a per diem rate starting at one penny for the first day, with each subsequent day's pay being twice the amount of the previous day's payment; thus, 1 cent on day one, 2 cents on day two, 4 cents on day three, 8 cents on day four, and so on throughout the thirty days of the contract. Which method of compensation would you choose, the generous lump sum or the progressive sequence of smaller numbers?

As a practical matter, there is little doubt about the alternative you should select. If you take the time to calculate the per diem rate through the thirty-day work life, you will find that the payment for the thirtieth day alone is $10,737,418.24. The aggregate amount of all the payments exceeds $20 million. Welcome to the world of geometric progressions.

This scenario was a fact situation presented to my grammar school class back in the 1940s to focus our attention on the subject of what is also called "geometric sequences" or "geometric series" of numbers. It is the mathematical equivalent of rolling a snowball across a freshly fallen snowfield to create the huge base for a large snowman. The "pennies-a-day" example made a big impression on me. There was no question about which alternative I would choose. It is now more than sixty years since I first heard that dramatic example of geometric progressions – and I have not had a single offer of employment on those terms. On the other hand, I have encountered geometric progressions that did not produce the anticipated results. One such progression was at the heart of Benjamin Franklin's famous codicil.

Benjamin Franklin was a brilliant man. On June 23, 1789, he wrote a codicil to his will. In the codicil, Franklin specified that 1,000 pounds sterling would fund a trust for the benefit of Philadelphia. The trust was to last for 200 years. The fund was to be used to make small loans to young, married craftsmen, at the favorable rate of five percent interest. Ben expected that, at the end of 100 years the money in the trust would be about £131,000, which would be pretty close to $524,000 in present-day currency. At the 100-year mark, the codicil directed that $400,000 should be used for "public works." Thereafter, the trust would continue for the rest of its 200-year life. If all went according to plan, there would be more than $16 million in the fund at the end of the year 200. At that point, approximately 75% of the fund was to be distributed to the government of Pennsylvania, and the remainder to "the inhabitants of Philadelphia."

All did not go according to plan. Enormous industrial growth and the emergence of large corporations virtually eliminated the craftsman class of workers that Franklin envisioned as the immediate beneficiaries of the fund. The demand for loans dried up. The money sat idle. At the end of 200 years, Franklin's trust had a value of only $2,256,952.05.

A less complicated geometric progression is the typical family tree. Think about it. Each of us has two parents, four grandparents, eight great-grandparents, and so on, *ad infinitum*, back into the murky past. Mathematically speaking, we can be certain that this ratio applied throughout all human experience. But when we trace our forbears back to the 30th generation, approximately to the year 1066 – the year of the Battle of Hastings – we calculate that 1,073,741,824 of our long forgotten forbears were alive and well. That is more than *one billion* persons. That seems impossible. That is impossible! That would mean we are related to nearly everyone who was alive in 1066, including the soldiers on both sides of the battle.

This is not a new thought. The subject has been frequently discussed by people who spend their time constructing family trees. They believe that the questionable geometric result is a consequence of inbreeding and its effect on genealogical sequences. Where people marry close relatives, the result is that one person often occupies multiple places on the family tree, thereby lowering the number of persons actually involved. For example, we expect that each of us has eight great-grandparents. However, where the parents are first cousins, the child will have only six great-grandparents because that child's parents share a common set of grandparents. In that circumstance, six persons occupy eight places on the tree. Most genealogists point to the well documented example of King Alfonso XII of Spain, who had only four great-grandparents instead of the usual eight. The mathematical effect of inbreeding is to reduce the number of persons on remote branches of the family tree. This effect is called "pedigree collapse."

Don't bet the house on a geometric progression – unless, of course, you happen to be related to the King of Spain.

This was one of my earliest poetical efforts — an attempt to capture the reality of an iconic neighborhood fixture that was fading into the past. Then, I learned just a few months ago that Ma Brown was the grandmother of one of my close friends. Otto Brown never mentioned it.

MA BROWN'S

A small, tin-roofed shed
Perched between two rows of houses,
One-half block before the school,
A refuge for the young.

A simple wooden counter,
Candy and long pretzel sticks,
Yellow mustard and a worn paintbrush,
The objects of our attention.

Ma Brown – the spittin' image of my grandmother,
Thin, wrinkled, gray hair pulled back,
Stays aloof from the young customers
Lest she give away the store.

JACK McLOUGHLIN

Our favorite cousin – an honor you shared with your sister Mary. You were a big kid when we were little kids. You were always there at gatherings of both Mom's and Dad's families. You were almost like an older brother.

As we grew older, you stayed one step ahead of us – going off to join the Air Force; and then displaying the good sense and maturity to marry Joan. Remember when you moved from your apartment in north Philadelphia up to St. Dominic's Parish? You made the mistake of asking who would drive the truck that you rented. I was not going to admit that I never drove a truck before. Oh well, we got there, didn't we? But it was an interesting trip.

It was also interesting when you suggested that I might want to play softball for the team that you used to hang out with at the Warnock Tavern in Logan. That experience introduced me to most of the taprooms in Philadelphia north of Allegheny Avenue. And the Warnock did have the worst draft beer in the Olney-Logan area. Fortunately, that softball season also gave me the opportunity to meet some of your buddies, such as Tom Welsh and George Pentram. They could play! And Tom Gola wasn't bad either, playing against us for the 50-50 Tavern.

Was that really fifty years ago? Where did the time go? Damned! You are old.

You focused on the family – you continued to stay a step ahead of us. John, Diane and Pat are great people – and now they are following in your footsteps. They could not have had better direction.

We got together two weeks ago and talked about the days gone by. Those days went too fast. Our talk went too fast. We cannot bring back the days gone by – but we will not forget them.

And we will not forget our favorite cousin.

THOUGHTS OF AN OLD ALUMNUS

My decision to attend St. Joseph's College was a last-minute thing in the summer of 1954. I was already registered at La Salle College when my brother suggested that I look at St. Joe's. During that last-minute look, I encountered the Registrar, Michael Boland, who persuaded me to make my future at St. Joe's.

It was an uncertain future to say the least. My study habits did not jibe with my electronic physics major and I dropped back into the Class of 1959, while changing my major, first to political science and then to economics. After graduation, I spent nearly four years as an officer in the United States Marine Corps and then took a job at the Redevelopment Authority of Philadelphia. After four years of evening classes at Temple University School of Law, I practiced law for more than forty years and then returned to St. Joe's as a member of the adjunct faculty in the political science department.

My view of Saint Joseph's reflects my background. I was just the second St. John to graduate from college (my brother Jack graduated from Penn in 1956). My Dad was a letter carrier, the son of iron-working immigrants from Newfoundland. My maternal grandfather was a foreman at the Stetson Hat Company. Many of my classmates had similar backgrounds. Their fathers were bus drivers, railroad workers, firemen, and policemen.

To me, St. Joseph's College was a place where the working people of Philadelphia could assure a college education of their children. Times have changed. Over the years, St. Joseph's has grown to university status and its tuition level is out of the reach of most working people. Our tuition was about $220 per semester at a time when $100 per week was a comfortable salary in the workplace. We commuted to school by public transportation. Only a handful of students lived on campus. Today, the tuition is about $42,000 per year, including room & board (virtually everyone is a resident student today), while the average letter carrier makes about $72,000 per year. It is a different world.

Saint Joseph's today is a world of substantial debt, mainly the loans needed to pay steep tuition bills. It is not a world that favors those who grow up in rowhouse neighborhoods. Saint Joseph's has changed.

GIVING BACK

In April 1969, I was on the verge of graduating from Temple University School of Law. It was an honor to be president of my evening division class, and that was undoubtedly the reason why I was chosen to be the class representative for the Levin-Sarner-Brown cram course that prepared us to take the Pennsylvania bar examination. As the class representative, I would attend the bar exam course free of charge. In the meanwhile, there were a number of administrative details that fell into my lap. I was not surprised when Ed Steinhouse, one of my classmates, caught my eye and signaled that he wanted to talk to me.

Ed and I were friends, albeit not particularly close. I held him in high regard as one of the brightest students in our class. His daytime occupation was as a teacher in the Philadelphia School District. In class, he was always well prepared, and his classroom responses were right on point. I assumed that Ed wanted to talk about some aspect of our graduation schedule. I had no idea that Ed was upset over a grievance that affected mainly the day school students. The dean of the law school had recently adopted strict rules to assure that all students attended the prescribed classes. Members of the administration monitored each class and submitted reports to the dean as to absences from those sessions. By and large, the night school students did not care about the monitoring. We just wanted to graduate, get our degree, and get the show on the road. On the other hand, the day school students took the monitoring as a personal affront. They used every opportunity to demonstrate their displeasure. They even bought T-shirts with their seat assignment number on the front and back.

Apparently, Ed intended to tell me that he had decided to demonstrate his dissatisfaction with the student monitoring policy by not contributing to the law school's fund-raising campaign. He began by stating:

"I have always been taught that we should sustain the institutions that sustained us,

but ...."

I have no idea what he said after that. I was so impressed with his clear and concise statement about sustaining institutions that sustained us, that I kept repeating that thought to myself. Ed continued to expound on his gripe against the administration, but I was no longer listening. A voice inside me kept repeating, *"we should sustain the institutions that sustained us."* What an exceptionally clear way of stating one's obligation to future generations. There was none of the ambiguity of that "giving back" approach that is voiced by many fund raisers. I never forgot it.

On the other hand, I suspect from this 1979 photo of Ed and I with Dr. Eldon Magaw that Ed changed his mind about contributing to sustain the law school.

THE OXFORD AND LOWER DUBLIN POOR HOUSE

In 1939, when we moved to the Mayfair neighborhood of Philadelphia, most of the land north of Cottman Avenue was undeveloped. You could stand on the front steps of our house at 3406 Chippendale Avenue and see open fields for nearly one-half mile up to Rhawn Street where there were a few scattered houses. About one-quarter mile to the west, on a low ridge line, was a horse farm that consisted of several red barns, a pasture, a hay field, a corn field and a large stone building. Carved into the archway above the main door of the stone building were the words, "Oxford and Lower Dublin Poor House." People generally called it "the poorhouse."

There is no longer a place called "Lower Dublin." But back in the 1700s, Lower Dublin Township included the area roughly north of Cottman Avenue up to about Grant Avenue, and between the Delaware River and the Montgomery County line.

For all practical purposes, Oxford Township included everything south of Cottman Avenue down to about Bridesburg. Although Oxford and Lower Dublin were both in Philadelphia County, they were outside the city limits. Oxford and Lower Dublin went out of existence in 1854 when the boundaries of the City of Philadelphia were consolidated with the boundaries of Philadelphia County.

Poorhouses – which were also called almshouses – were an integral part of Pennsylvania's original public welfare system. As early as 1705, the Pennsylvania Assembly recognized a responsibility of government to provide for the poor and the indigent. The Assembly directed justices of the peace annually to elect two or more Overseers of the Poor who were authorized "to levy a tax of one penny per pound (sterling) on real and personal property of citizens of the township, and four shillings per head on all citizens not otherwise rated." The money collected through this "poor tax" was "to be used for the relief of poor, indigent and impotent persons inhabiting within the township."[1]

After the founding of the United States, Pennsylvania continued to meet its responsibility to the weakest of its citizens through an evolving series of public welfare laws. Over time, the titles of the governing public agencies changed from Overseers of

---

[1]   Lawrence, Charles, *History of the Philadelphia Almshouses and Hospitals.* (1905).

the Poor to "Directors of the Poor," "Guardians of the Poor," "Bureau of Charities and Correction," and finally "Department of Public Welfare."

The ranks of the Pennsylvania poor were plentiful. Included were elderly persons, victims of bank failures and other economic disasters, disabled persons, immigrants far from home, persons with mental difficulties, and persons who, for whatever the reason, were unable to take care of themselves.

Pennsylvania taxpayers two centuries ago were much like taxpayers today; they recognized a responsibility to the poor and the indigent, but they were wary of creating a welfare class that would be dependent on state handouts. Taxpayers wanted poorhouses to be closely monitored to make sure that they served only the "deserving" poor. A stigma was attached to residents of poorhouses. They were required to register in "poor books." In some locations, they were required to wear the letter "P" on the sleeves of their clothing. Frequently, where poorhouses were built there were also houses of employment where the poorhouse residents were required to work. On the other side of the coin, there was a tendency on the part of some poorhouse managers to misappropriate poor tax monies for their personal use. The managers of those facilities required constant supervision. It was not a perfect system.

Acting under a law adopted in 1807, the Townships of Oxford and Lower Dublin appointed a Board of Overseers of the

Poor and began collecting a poor tax. The Overseers decided to carry out their responsibilities through a poorhouse. Although the exact details of their decision are not presently available, it appears that they purchased an existing farm of approximately 146 acres. The north boundary of the farm was one-third mile along Pennypack Creek from Sandy Run east to the old dam that later generations called "the waterfall." The farm buildings were at the north end of the property, nestled against the woods that sloped downhill to the creek. The farm was accessible by an unimproved road that extended from Rhawn Street south along the route of the present-day Rowland Avenue to where Sheffield Street is located, and then west to the farm. Another unimproved road ran south to what is now Ryan Avenue at about Brous Street.

In 1833, the Directors of the Poor sold the water rights to 2.5 acres along Pennypack Creek to Samuel Comly, who then owned the Calico Printing Works, including the dam near Rhawn Street. After Comly sold the business, it became known as the Pennepack Printing Works. In 1854, the poorhouse effectively became part of the City of Philadelphia when the boundaries of the city and the county were consolidated and the city absorbed Oxford and Lower Dublin Townships. Significantly, title to the poorhouse real estate remained vested in the Directors of the Poor.

In the late 1850s, the poorhouse was destroyed by fire. In 1868, the city fathers, in their wisdom determined that the poorhouse site would be an excellent place for a proposed new prison. The price was right. With the city and county boundaries consolidated, the city assumed that it already owned the land. Fortunately for those of us who later made our homes in this area, the City Solicitor issued a legal opinion that title to the real estate remained vested in the Directors of the Poor, and the property could not be used for prison purposes without the consent of the voters. The city fathers were not willing to put the issue to a democratic vote.

The overseers decided to build a new poorhouse. Charles W. Harrison, a Philadelphia merchant who owned a farm in Byberry, north of Red Lion Road, was chairman of the building committee. George Fox, the owner of Foxdale Farm which was located between the poorhouse and the present day Frankford Avenue, was also instrumental in the decision, as was Theodore A. Hermann, a Holmesburg druggist. In about 1868, a large stone building was constructed to meet the needs of the indigent. It cost a whopping $30,000![2]

The poorhouse was designed to provide food and shelter for one hundred persons. The main floor of the stone building provided a studio and a shop, as well as kitchen facilities, bathrooms and bedrooms. The second and third floors contained

---

[2]   Willits, Samuel C., *A History of Lower Dublin Academy etc.,* (1885) (Published by Trustees of Lower Dublin Academy 2009).

more bedrooms. Outside, there were chicken coops, a springhouse and a vegetable garden in addition to a large hay field and a cornfield. The farm buildings consisted of a carriage house, two barns and a corncrib.

In 1883, the Board of Commissioners of Public Charities inspected the poorhouse and found that it housed 57 persons. Most of the residents were elderly. Twenty residents were foreign born. Men and women occupied opposite wings of the building and had separate exercise yards. Registers for heat and ventilation, bathrooms, and other necessities were available.

Anna Hallowell and Catherine K. Meredith, members of the County Visitors Committee, reported as follows:

> "The poor-house we found to be properly an alms-house, that is, a refuge for the aged and decrepit poor. Among the inmates we did not see one able-bodied person, though several of the elderly men and women seemed capable of doing a little labor about the house and farm. The steward explained the absence of able-bodied women, by the resolution of the board of guardians, a year or more ago, to keep no children in the poor-house, but to put every child coming to them into the Pauline Home, at Germantown…."

In about 1905, the City came up with another potential use for the poorhouse property. They proposed to use it as the site for new facilities to treat the insane. Again the city fathers were reluctant to submit their idea to the voters; and like the proposed prison, the mental health facilities were built elsewhere.

In the 1930s, during the Great Depression, government construction projects by the Civil Works Administration (CWA) and the Works Progress Administration (WPA) improved the area surrounding the poorhouse. Bridle paths were developed along Pennypack Creek. The "boathouse" swimming area was opened just downhill from the poorhouse pasture. The old dam was rebuilt and became a waterfall. A drainage system was constructed to carry water from Sandy Run and surrounding storm sewers into Pennypack Creek. Spurred by these improvements, private housing development sprung up on the land adjacent to Rowland Avenue. The prices of those houses –$5,000 for a middle-of-the-row house and about $7,000 for a corner property – were high for the Depression era. Times were changing, and the old poorhouse was coming to the end of its trail.

Pennsylvania's welfare laws were also changing. In 1938, the Pennsylvania Legislature abolished the Directors of the Poor and transferred title to their real estate to the City of Philadelphia. The poorhouse was shut down. Its residents were sent to Philadelphia's Home for the Indigent at Riverview. A caretaker was assigned to maintain the poorhouse property and continue the operation of the farm.

Vested with the power of ownership, the city fathers came up with another new idea for the poorhouse grounds. In 1940, they proposed to build a public housing project using mainly federal funds. The city tried to force its plan on the public, treating it as a *fait accompli*. Local residents rose up and challenged the proposal. Their real estate taxes were among the highest in the city, and they were angry. Meetings were held at the Mayfair Baseball Field at the corner of Rowland and Ryan Avenues. Homeowners made it clear that they would cast their votes against any city official who supported this proposal. Confronted with strong public opposition, the city backed down. The housing project was built elsewhere.

In 1942, the country was at war, and food was in short supply. The open land between the poorhouse and Rowland Avenue, from Shelmire to Sheffield Streets, was made available to the public for use as vegetable gardens. They were called "Victory Gardens." It was part of a nationwide effort to supplement the country's food supply. Each garden was about the size of an average rowhouse living room (about 14'x15'). The most common crops were tomatoes, lettuce, cabbage, carrots and radishes. Some of the neighborhood gardeners were more talented than others. They built elaborate trellises and also grew string beans, lima beans and peas.

Philip McMahon tending his victory garden on the Poorhouse grounds near Rowland Avenue in 1942.

Jim McMahon, who lived on the 3500 block of Chippendale Avenue, still recalls his father regularly walking two blocks with a hoe and a rake to take care of his victory garden. The photo above shows behind Philip McMahon the stakes that marked the boundaries of his and nearby plots. Nationwide, victory gardens produced an amount of fresh vegetables equal to the total commercial production of those items.[3] Some of the victory gardens continued to be used for several years after the victory was won.

In 1946, the large two-level barn was destroyed in a spectacular fire. At that time, the only occupants of the poorhouse were the caretaker, Logan Jamieson, and members of his family. One of those family members was Charles Durr, who had recently returned from wartime service in the Marine Corps. When the fire was discovered, Charles ran to the stables  on the ground level of the blazing barn. He took off his shirt, soaked it in water and draped the shirt over the head of one of the frightened horses. One-by-one, Durr led the horses outside to the safety of the pasture. An article in *The Mayfair Times* described Charles Durr as a hero.

3   www.livinghistoryfarm.org/farminginthe40s/crops_02.html

Charles' brother Ron Durr, who now lives in Ambler, was eleven years old at the time of the fire. Ron was fond of the horses: a big black horse named Smokey, and a brown horse named Dixie. The horses were owned by Peggy Mayers, a resident of Frankford. Durr recalls that one-half of the hay grown at the poorhouse was sent to Holmesburg Prison; although he does not know why that was the case. Closer to home, Durr still recalls the blackberries that grew wild around the edge of the pasture. The photo above shows the view north from one of the upstairs bedrooms (circa 1946). Ron Durr's sketches of the poorhouse building and grounds are attached to the end of this article.

Despite the devastating fire, the ground level of the barn continued to be used to stable the horses. Also, it was an attractive, albeit dangerous place for local children to play. That danger was brought home one afternoon when a neighborhood boy lost an eye in an accident that occurred in the burned-out stables. The old farm was becoming what lawyers call "an attractive nuisance." It would have to go.

In the meanwhile, the city came up with another proposed use for the poorhouse grounds. The city proposed that the site be used for a needed public high school for northeast Philadelphia. A major obstacle to this proposal was that a substantial parcel of land at the northwest corner of Rowland and Ryan Avenues was owned by Mayfair A.A., a community organization that maintained three baseball fields, a small wading pool and a playground at that site. Mayfair A.A. was reluctant to go along with the city's proposal because it would leave the community without its athletic fields and, besides, the city had a long record of changing its priorities. The property might be used for something other than a school.

After negotiations, the parties reached agreement. The city gave assurance that the property would be used for school purposes. Moreover, the city assured that the athletic facilities would be available for use by the public. With those assurances, Mayfair A.A. agreed to the proposal and conveyed its land to the city.

The high school was built near the intersection of Rowland and Ryan Avenues. John Gindhart, president of Mayfair A.A., was employed as the watchman for the construction project. The farm buildings were demolished, and the open ground was graded for use as athletic fields. The old stone poorhouse was the last to go. Abraham Lincoln High School opened in 1950 – before construction was completed. During that first school year, a fire erupted in the old poorhouse. Afterward, the poorhouse building was demolished. Lincoln High's main baseball diamond was built just north of the site of the old poorhouse building. The third base line was aligned parallel to the axis of the old stone building.

In 2009-2010, a new high school building was constructed to the west of the original high school. Lincoln High seems to be moving closer to the Poorhouse site. The photo below shows the site of the old Poorhouse as it appeared in May 2010.

Today, the poorhouse property is a 146-acre campus for secondary education. The campus includes Abraham Lincoln High School, the Austin Meehan Middle School, and a large expanse of athletic fields. It is a tribute to the foresight of the overseers who originally purchased the property, and to the initiative of the local citizens who exercised their civic responsibilities and resisted a series of undesirable ideas thrust upon them by municipal officials over the years. After more than two centuries, the Oxford and Lower Dublin Poor House continues to serve the community very well.

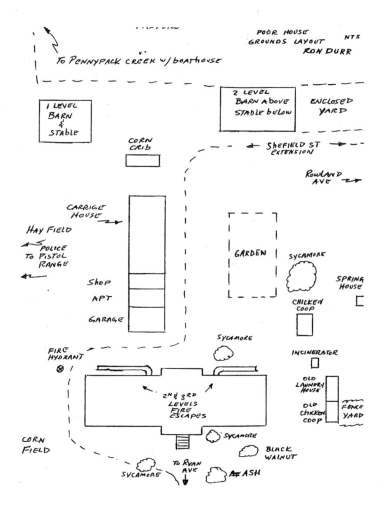

To Pennypack Creek w/boathouse

POOR HOUSE
GROUNDS LAYOUT   NTS
RON DURR

1 LEVEL BARN & STABLE

2 LEVEL BARN ABOVE STABLE BELOW

ENCLOSED YARD

CORN CRIB

SHEFIELD ST EXTENSION

ROWLAND AVE

CARRIGE HOUSE

HAY FIELD

POLICE TO PISTOL RANGE

GARDEN

SYCAMORE

SPRING HOUSE

SHOP

APT

GARAGE

CHICKEN COOP

FIRE HYDRANT

SYCAMORE

INCINERATOR

OLD LAUNDRY HOUSE

2ND & 3RD LEVELS FIRE ESCAPES

OLD CHICKEN COOP

FENCE YARD

CORN FIELD

SYCAMORE

BLACK WALNUT

SYCAMORE

To RYAN AVE

ASH

240

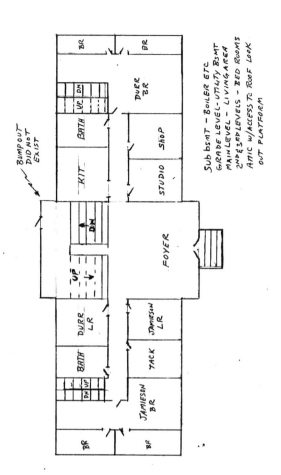

Drawings by Ron Durr (2010)

THE EDWIN FORREST HOME AT SPRINGBROOK

Springbrook was the name given to a 111-acre property

FORREST HOME, HOLMESBURG.

in Lower Dublin Township, overlooking the Delaware River. The perimeter of Springbrook measured nearly two miles. It was named for the clear springs and the stream that ran near its northeastern

EDWIN FORREST HOME.
Holmesburg.

boundary, down toward the river. In the early 1800s, Springbrook was an ideal location for wealthy businessmen who wanted a country estate to avoid the oppressive heat and the inevitable scourge of yellow fever in the Philadelphia summer.

In approximately 1810, Josiah W. Gibbs, one of the owners of the Pennepack Print Works, built a three-story roughcast yellow stone mansion at the crest of the hill. Like most river view mansions, the carriage entrance faced away from the river and toward the highway, in this case toward the Bristol Turnpike which we now call Frankford Avenue. It was a stately mansion with a colonial doorway and two large pillars that supported a small porch that covered the entrance. Inside the mansion, a wide corridor extended from the front door straight through the house to the door on the river side. Overlooking the river was a veranda that offered an outstanding view thanks to the gradual slope of the terrain and a wide expanse of open lawn.

In 1837, Caleb Cope, a silk wholesaler, who also was a director of the Second Bank of the United States, and president of Philadelphia Saving Fund Society, purchased Springbrook from Gibbs. Cope developed the property as an arboretum. There were flowers, fruit trees, grape vines and berries in abundance. Greenhouses outnumbered barns at Springbrook. One of the greenhouses was situated at the southwest wing of the mansion and served as a conservatory for the rare plants. It extended from the house in a southerly direction, and was encircled by a pathway that looped around to the veranda. Serpentine walkways meandered through colorful gardens, by a small lake and past exotic tropical plants. Local historian Samuel C. Willits noted that the display of Victoria Regia, a large water lily found in Central and South America, made this "villa known throughout the floral world and induced hundreds to come, some from long distances to see it in bloom."

George H. Stuart, a businessman who is mainly remembered as the first president of the Philadelphia YMCA, bought Springbrook from Mr. Cope. Stuart called it his "garden estate."

In 1865, Springbrook attracted the interest of Edwin Forrest, America's first great Shakespearean actor. A native Philadelphian born of modest means, Forrest found his way into the theater at the age of eleven years. He performed in an era before the development of electricity, when theaters were poorly lighted and had no sound amplification systems. Forrest had a muscular physique – the result of intensive physical exercise. Also, he had an exceptional memory and a magnificent voice – a voice that

Edwin Forrest at age twenty.

not only could be heard clearly in every part of the theater, but one that also conveyed a wide range of emotions, whether uttered in a whisper or a roar. He was a sensation both in America and Europe. After more than forty years in the theatrical limelight, he was a wealthy man. In October 1865, Forrest purchased the Springbrook property at public auction for the sum of $91,000. He had big plans for this country estate.

Springbrook was to be the centerpiece of Edwin Forrest's will. He directed his executors to create a nonprofit corporation to manage Springbrook as a permanent residence for actors who, by reason of age or disability could no longer earn a living in the theater. In contrast to township old age homes, such as the Oxford and Lower Dublin Poor House located three-quarters of a mile to the west, Forrest's home would be a luxury dwelling. The poor house was designed to shelter one hundred persons; it was like a grey stone army barracks. At Springbrook the number of residents was limited to twelve at any one time. Each resident had a private room that could be furnished as he or she saw fit; and each received a regular allowance sufficient to buy clothing and provide pocket money. Springbrook was a horticultural jewel that invited its residents to walk among the scenic flowers. The estate's carriage was available to transport the elderly residents to church and other venues. It was a place where all their physical and medical needs would be met without cost. It even had burial space available in West Laurel Hill Cemetery, where the gravestone identifies the deceased as "Guests of Edwin Forrest."

The only obligation of Springbrook's residents was to participate in two celebrations each year: (1) the April 23rd birthday of William Shakespeare, and (2) the Fourth of July birthday of the

United States. The Board of Managers added a third celebration. On each March 9th, they celebrated the birthday of Edwin Forrest. These celebrations were professional theatrical performances. Actors and actresses who were appearing in the major Philadelphia theaters were invited to participate in the festivities, as were those of the New York Lyceum Theater. Many of them accepted the invitation. Professional musicians were hired. Outsiders and insiders joined together to present dramatic readings and scenes from well known plays. These celebrations were attended not only by the residents, but by the Board of Managers and high-profile visitors from the entertainment world, people like Ethel Barrymore and escape artist Harry Houdini, in addition to many contemporary theatrical performers whose names are no longer recognized by the general public. In 1894, on the 330th birthday of Shakespeare, a train from Broad Street Station carried 500 invited guests to Holmesburg Junction where they boarded coaches for the remaining part of their journey to Springbrook. After a reception and lunch in the mansion, the guests attended a show of music and stage performances in a large white tent set on the lawn.

The 100th birthday of Edwin Forrest was special. There were decorations, distinguished guests, festive meals, and a visit to the grave of Edwin Forrest at Old St. Paul's Episcopal Church on Third Street, south of Walnut, two blocks from the site of his birth. New York and Philadelphia newspapers carried headline coverage of the celebration, including photographs of the Mayor of Philadelphia with Kate Ludlow Littell, the oldest female resident of the Home.

The name of the residence was the "Edwin Forrest Home." The Edwin Forrest Home sounds like an asylum; but that is the name Forrest gave it. Other words of the plan were equally inept. For example, a home for "superannuated actors" is a  mouthful; "decayed actors" is even worse. He called the residents "inmates." In all probability, the word "home" was required by the applicable law so as to assure that the residence would be treated as a charity. Still, it is clear that Forrest had in mind the use of the word "home" in its best sense. In contrast to Stephen Girard's walled-in fortress on Corinthian Avenue, Forrest directed his executors to assure that the enclosure surrounding Springbrook would be low enough to allow a five-foot tall person on the sidewalk to see into the estate. It would be a place where dramatic acting was taught.

Forrest moved his 6,000-book library into Springbrook. Additional books were donated to the library by other actors and authors. The mansion was furnished with artwork and memorabilia that he cherished. Thomas Ball's larger-than-life white marble statue of Forrest in the title role of Shakespeare's Coriolanus was placed in the main corridor, at the foot of the center staircase. Also in the main corridor were a bust of Shakespeare and a variety of paintings of great actors. The ground floor of the mansion included sitting rooms, a dining room, and the library. The rooms were large, with high ceilings, and furnished with hand-carved mahogany and black walnut tables and chairs. The mansion was decorated throughout with daggers and swords, and other theatrical memorabilia. Meals were served family style in the formal dining room. Springbrook was the kind of home where Edwin Forrest would have liked to live.

Edwin Forrest died on December 12, 1872; and his will was filed one month later. The Edwin Forrest Home was promptly incorporated, but remained dormant until the estate's accounting was approved by the Orphans' Court. Forrest's former wife, Catherine Sinclair, asserted a claim against the estate for dower (the common law right of a surviving spouse to set aside the provisions of a will, and take her share of the estate). Prior to his death, Forrest had pursued a long, drawn-out, expensive and highly publicized lawsuit against his wife, alleging adultery – and he lost the case. When he paid the verdict for court-ordered alimony, he thought all claims by or against Catherine were resolved. He was wrong. The executors paid Catherine an additional $100,000 to settle her claims against the estate. In the meanwhile, people claiming to be relatives of Forrest also sought pieces of the estate. An author claimed payment for a biography that he had not yet completed. Playwrights sought royalties from theatrical works that they previously sold to Forrest. Finally, on June 12, 1875, the first accounting was approved by the court, clearing the way for Forrest's executors to sell the estate's other properties and to prepare Springbrook for its new residents. On November 7, 1876, the first resident entered Springbrook.

The Edwin Forrest Home met the goals that were set for it by Forrest's will. It was managed by a seven-member blue ribbon Board of Managers that included the Mayor of Philadelphia, Forrest's executors, and trusted persons who held leadership positions in other Philadelphia institutions. The home was an attractive facility; and it was well maintained and managed by a competent staff that outnumbered the residents.

Actors were a segment of society that often had no deep roots in the communities they served and lacked the wherewithal for retirement. In the theater business of that era, nearly all the proceeds were divided between the star of the show and the owner of the theater. Supporting actors received little compensation. Moreover, there was a fairly widespread public prejudice against actors, particularly after the assassination of Abraham Lincoln. That prejudice even impaired the ability of many actors to arrange for their burials.

In fifty years of operation at Springbrook, the Edwin Forrest Home provided sanctuary to an estimated eighty residents, giving them a comfortable lifestyle that was beyond their wildest dreams. The residents were a cross-section of the theatrical world. Some examples are as follows:

- Kate Ludlow Littell was once a dark-haired leading lady of the Broadway stage, pursued by many admirers. As years passed, her name dropped lower and lower on the marquee. No longer were there crowds of young men waiting for her at the stage door after the show. But now Kate was in her nineties and once again she was a leading lady, albeit a white-haired leading lady at Springbrook where the oldest actress was deemed to be the queen of the house.

- John Jack was an actor known as "Captain Jack" in deference to the rank he achieved in the Civil War. He was wounded at the battle of Bull Run while serving with the Second Pennsylvania Volunteers. Captain Jack and his wife Annie Firmin were among the few husband-wife stage teams to reside at Springbrook. He often played the role of Falstaff in scenes with fellow resident Charles J. Fyffe.

- George W. Barnum was both an actor and a director on the New York stage, but he may be better remembered as an umpire in major league baseball. He was the first umpire to wear cleated shoes, so as to keep up with the pace of the game.

• Charles J. Fyffe appeared on stage in Canada, South America and the West Indies, in addition to his roles in the United States. He worked in support of a number of stars, including Edwin Forrest and Edwin Booth. In 1893, he became the unofficial librarian and historian of Springbrook. Fyffe also assisted a number of Holmesburg civic and social groups in their charitable efforts, including theatrical performances to raise funds for the relief of victims of the great Galveston hurricane disaster of 1900.

One thing that Edwin Forrest did not fully anticipate was change. The local government changed. A dozen years before Forrest bought Springbrook, Lower Dublin Township went out of existence when Philadelphia's city limits were extended to coincide with the county boundaries. Changes also occurred along the Delaware River. A line of railroad track was installed near the river, extending from Trenton to Kensington Station, a few miles south of Springbrook. Railroads grew in importance and railroad traffic grew in volume, especially when the cross-town tracks made it possible for trains going past Springbrook to continue on through center city, to and from points south. While older businesses in the northeast used power from mills on Pennypack Creek, railroads now brought coal, oil, and electricity to power the industries that people called "the workshop of the world." Additional sets of railroad tracks and railroad sidings were installed. Gradually, the land between Springbrook and the river became an industrial area. In 1896, the foreboding

Holmesburg Prison took its place next to the House of Correction and the Philadelphia Home for the Indigent as Springbrook's northern neighbors.

In 1922, the new Frankford elevated transit line was poised to increase the flow of people into the neighborhoods surrounding Springbrook. Farmland west of Frankford Avenue was being sold for residential development. The city published plans for new streets, and even proposed streets to run through the Springbrook property. Meanwhile, the inflation that followed World War I was draining the treasury of the Edwin Forrest Home. A benefit performance at Philadelphia's Forrest Theater raised $4,500 for the Home. Also, the mansion was out of date. It was an eighteenth century dwelling in the early twentieth century, lighted by oil lamps and lacking in modern plumbing and heating. Springbrook was no longer the country estate that Forrest knew. The Board of Managers looked for a new site for the Edwin Forrest Home. In 1926, Springbrook was sold for $600,000 to real estate developers who demolished the mansion and built exactly the type of high density housing that Forrest's Board of Managers feared. After a two-year rental of the Castor mansion on Solly Avenue, the Edwin Forrest Home moved to new quarters on Parkside Avenue, next to the Bala Golf Club in Fairmount Park.

The Edwin Forrest Home continued operations on Parkside Avenue until 1986, when additional changing circumstances led to its dissolution. Changes in the entertainment business, actors' equity contracts, and changes in social security laws resulted in actors being better prepared to deal with the financial perils of old age. Increasingly, the persons applying for admission to the Edwin Forrest Home were those in need of nursing home care, and the Edwin Forrest Home was not designed to provide that expensive level of healthcare. The Board of Managers decided to dissolve the Edwin Forrest Home and merge it with the Actors' Fund of America, a similar but larger organization headquartered in Englewood, New Jersey. The property of the Edwin Forrest Home was sold and more than one million dollars was transferred to the Actors' Fund of America. A wing of the nursing home of the Actors Fund in Englewood is named in honor of Edwin Forrest.

In retrospect, Edwin Forrest's will achieved a level of significance matched only by Benjamin Franklin's 200-year trust for the citizens of Philadelphia, and Stephen Girard's school for "poor white male" orphans. Forrest's biographer makes the following observation:

"Men have sought to perpetuate their memories with hospitals, libraries, schools and statues; few have achieved the kind of living immortality, an unbroken link with the past, a daily reminder of the benefactor's generosity, that Edwin Forrest achieved in the creation of his Home for 'decayed actors.'"[4]

Marble statue of Edwin Forrest in the lobby of the Walnut Street Theater, Philadelphia.

The Edwin Forrest Home provided luxury retirement housing for more than one hundred supporting actors over the course of 110 years – the first 50 years of which were at Springbrook.

Throughout Philadelphia, memorabilia of Edwin Forrest remain on display. Paintings of Forrest by famous artists and photographs by Matthew Brady appear in museums. A gravestone on the Edwin Forrest Home's plot in West Laurel Hill Cemetery bears the inscription: "All the World's a Stage, and all Men and Women Merely Actors." The 7-foot marble statue of Forrest that once dominated the main hall of

---

4   Moody, Richard. *Edwin Forrest: First Star of the American Stage* (A.A. Knopf 1960) at 5.

Springbrook now graces the lobby of the Walnut Street Theatre, the site of Forrest's first professional performance in 1820.

In contrast to the availability of Forrest memorabilia, it is almost impossible to find or appreciate the remains of Springbrook in northeast Philadelphia. It takes less than an hour to walk its perimeter: From Cottman and Frankford Avenues east to Ditman Street, north to Sheffield Avenue, west to Frankford Avenue, and back to Cottman. It is a large area. The streets are narrow. The houses seem to close in on you.

One of the present-day landmarks is the Mayfair Diner on Frankford Avenue at Bleigh Street. Two blocks or so behind the diner is the Edwin Forrest Elementary School. It is located very close to the site of the old Springbrook mansion. However, there is no view of the river. The view is obstructed by block after block of two-story rowhouses. There are no longer any springs, no brook, no lakes, and no serpentine walkways. There are some flower gardens scattered around the rowhouses, but there are no greenhouses, no Victoria Regia, and no admiring crowds of flower lovers. On the 111-acre property where a dozen elderly actors once passed their remaining years in comfortable repose, today an estimated six thousand citizens meet the challenges of their everyday lives. Few of the present-day residents are aware of the role their neighborhood once played in the life of the American theater.